Leading Through Succession:

Why Pastoral Leadership

is the Key to a Healthy

Transition

By

Andrew Flowers

Dedicated to my mentor and friend Pastor Henry Tucker, who modeled humble leadership.

Table of Contents

Part 1
Diagnosing Transition Pains

Part 2
Making Transitions Healthier

Part 1

Diagnosing Transition Pains

Chapter 1

WHERE DOES IT HURT?

About a year ago I started having horrible pain in my feet. It got to the point that I could barely walk. The doctors diagnosed me with plantar fasciitis and offered the usual treatments. But things only got worse. The pain spread to my hips and then my back and then my neck. The doctor thought the pain was due to the change in the way I walked or too much exercise or maybe the way I slept.

Finally a referral to a different doctor led to the right diagnosis. I had something called Ankylosing Spondylitis; a form of arthritis that often shows up in men my age. The disease is tough to catch because the symptoms often resemble other ailments. But with the right diagnosis I was immediately given the right treatment and started down the road to recovery.

There is a rapidly growing area of disease within the church world today. It is the source of significant suffering for churches and pastors. It is a problem that has been improperly diagnosed and improperly treated for years. But the reality of the problem is felt in every denomination and every corner of the church. The problem is failed pastoral transitions.

Feeling the Pain

I first felt the pain of a failed pastoral transition during my college years. When I left for school my home church was growing and thriving. New people where coming to faith, a new worship facility was being planned, and each area of ministry was active and alive. It was a healthy church.

The senior pastor had served the church faithfully for nearly 20 years and was nearing retirement. The congregation knew that a change in leadership was inevitable. The church had a great board, seasoned pastoral staff, and plenty of financial resources. It seemed like they had everything they needed to handle the transition well.

Over the course of the next seven years I watched as the church that I loved shrank from 500 members to barely 100. It started with a struggle for leadership that resulted in a church split. Then the church shrank more with the arrival of a new senior pastor. After two years of frustration that pastor left and another pastor was brought in. His tenure didn't last much longer and the attrition grew worse.

As I talked with friends and family back home I was grieved to see how much the church had lost. The loss in morale caused a number of people to leave and attend other churches. That resulted in a loss of momentum and the ministries began to dry up. The church faced a huge loss in money and the debts began to mount. In less than a decade I saw a vibrant, thriving, growing church come very close to death, primarily because the transition from one senior pastor to the next was handled so poorly.[1]

During my seminary years I began to discover that this problem was not unique to my home church. I interacted with a number of churches that were still picking up the pieces after their beloved pastor had left. It seemed like my classmates and professors all had stories to share that mirrored my own.

But the deepest pain that I felt came from watching my buddies graduate from seminary and head with excitement into their first ministry jobs only to be chewed up and spit out. I saw friends who moved from one church to the next and then finally just give up and leave ministry altogether.

I was disheartened to learn that it is not uncommon for seminary graduates to struggle to settle in a ministry role. Pastor Gary Pinion writes about this issue in his 2006 book, *Crushed: The Perilous Side of Ministry*. He says, "Eighty percent of seminary and Bible school graduates who enter the ministry will leave the ministry within the first five years."[2] Something seems to be horribly wrong with the process of appointing pastors.

My seminary colleagues were men who had a heart to serve God. There was no reason they had to fail. My home church was healthy

---

[1] A more detailed case study of this church can be found in the appendix.

[2] Gary L. Pinion, *Crushed: The Perilous Journey Called Ministry* (Springfield, MO: 21st Century, 2006.), 57.

and strong, it didn't have to fall apart. What could have been done differently to prevent the loss of ministry and morale?

After seminary I applied for a number of pastoral positions. The one that excited me the most was a senior pastor position at the other Baptist church in my own home town. The senior pastor was retiring after 37 years of service!

I turned to my professors for letters of recommendation and for prayer and advice. One of them bluntly advised me to just run! "You will be the sacrificial lamb!" he said. "It is very rare for the man who immediately follows a long-time pastor to survive."

His advice came from a heart of love for me and decades of experience in the church. He spoke truth to me that day. But I thought the same thing that thousands of other eager seminary graduates have thought: "I can handle it. It won't happen to me. It will be different this time." I moved forward with equal parts optimism and arrogance.

At the age of 30 I was called to be the new senior pastor and took the reins from the man who had been there for almost four decades. As I head towards my eleventh year as senior pastor, I praise God that I was not a sacrificial lamb! I realize that my success has had very little to do with me.[3]

---

[3] A more detailed case study of my experience can be found in the appendix.

The pain felt by churches and pastors during a failed transition is very real and very common. My goal in this book is to think through some of the reasons our current methods of succession planning aren't working and offer a more effective option.

Identifying the Symptoms

In the book *Next* the trauma caused during pastoral transitions is referred to as "The epidemic that no one wants to talk about."[4] Failure to successfully pass the baton has left countless churches and pastors in ruins. It affects both small churches and large churches alike. When a transition does go badly, the blame is often pointed in the wrong direction. The end result is a growing problem within the church world that has not been properly diagnosed and is not being properly treated.

Perhaps part of the reason that a proper diagnosis is so elusive is because the symptoms mask the real problem. The church fails to identify the real problem because the whole situation is so filled with confusion and emotion. The process unfolds over the course of months and sometimes years. At the end the church is a smoldering mess and it's not sure why.

Here's the scenario: The old pastor leaves, the new pastor comes, and then everything falls apart. What happened to cause things to go

[4] Vanderbloemen, William, Warren Bird. *Next*. Grand Rapids, MI: Baker Books, 2014, 128.

so wrong? Who gets the blame? Usually the blame falls in one of three directions.

It's the New Pastor's Fault!

Often the blame lands on the incoming pastor. He's just too different. He's not as good as the former minister. He does everything wrong. He's the reason people are leaving and giving is down. Personality conflicts and power struggles lead to mounting frustration. Because the new pastor doesn't understand the history and culture of that church he unintentionally steps on landmines that he didn't even know where there. Eventually the new pastor resigns and moves on. It's easy to place the bulk of the blame on his shoulders.

However, it's not uncommon for churches to go through two or three sacrificial lambs before someone is able to stick. Not all of them are bad pastors, and many of them are able to transition to another church and thrive. It isn't really all their fault.

It's The Search Committee's Fault!

Sometimes the blame lands on the search committee. They were the ones who recommended the new minister. They should have screened him better. They didn't understand the culture of the church. They are responsible for the decline. If they would have done their job the church wouldn't be suffering.

Many of the books written on the topic of pastoral succession are about how to build a better search committee. Moreover, the consensus among many church leaders I speak with is that if the search committee does its job right a bad fit is avoidable. However, perhaps the search committee is not to blame. It is usually made up of men and women who love God and love the church. They commit the process to prayer. They take their time. They can do everything by the book and still end up with a replacement that doesn't work out.

It's Those People's Fault!

Often the church becomes divided with some people supportive of the new pastor and some opposed to him. The two groups blame each other for the church decline. "Those petty, shallow people have ruined the church!" Often a chunk of people leave to start their own church or attend somewhere else. It's easy to blame the people who aren't around anymore.

Disunity within the church is not a new thing, but it is still not the main reason why transitions fail. There is a factor that is far more significant than the personality of the new pastor, or the efficiency of the search committee, or the unity of the congregation. There is a key ingredient to church health that is often missing from the process. The leadership of the outgoing pastor.

Searching for Solutions

There are a number of factors that make the search for solutions difficult. Pastoral transitions that fail are filled with frustration and anger. It can be hard to see through the emotion and properly identify what went wrong. Transitions that succeed are rarely studied to determine what went right. Shifts in the culture make old methods less reliable, but the church is notorious for taking too long to adjust to these shifts.

In order to find answers I spent time talking to various denomination leaders. These people serve as the pastor to the pastors. They overseer multiple churches and have first-hand experience with walking congregations through the transition process. As outside agents, they are less likely to point the blame in the wrong direction and better able to identify the root cause of transitional failures.

In addition, I conducted my own case studies. I interviewed a number of people from two small churches in the same rural town. Both churches went through the process of replacing their senior pastor. One of those churches struggled greatly in the years that followed and the other experienced a seamless transition. I wanted to investigate the factors that lead to success.

Finally, I searched the Scriptures for help. The Word of God is not silent on this issue. There are some principles from the Bible that can help guide the process of pastoral succession. God doesn't give us the detailed blueprint that we might want, but there is a pattern that emerges from a study of biblical examples of leadership transitions. We will look to the relationship between Moses and Joshua, Elijah and Elisha, and Paul and Timothy to help identify important leadership qualities that pave the way to a smooth transition.

Every church is different and every transition is unique. The greatest challenge in making the right diagnosis and suggesting a helpful treatment is that there are so many variables in every situation. There are different ecclesiastical structures, different reasons that pastors have for leaving, different search methods, and different cultures. No two churches are alike!

However, even with all the variables, my research shows that there is one factor that keeps rising to the surface. My purpose here is not to address every variable, but to highlight the one constant that is found in almost every successful pastoral transition. Vanderbloemen and Bird identify this factor in their book about pastoral succession. "In the end, most of the success of a pastoral transition rises and falls on the shoulders of the outgoing pastor."[5]

---

[5] Vanderbloemen and Bird, 57.

My prayer is that this study will help pastors understand the huge influence they have over the future health of their church. We must begin to accept a measure of responsibility for helping the leader who will come after us. I hope that what follows will help you better understand the important pastoral leadership role that God has called you to.

Chapter 2

OBSTACLES TO DIAGNOSIS

In the past year I've gotten to know my rheumatologist pretty well. It took a number of visits and a bunch of different tests before she was able to accurately diagnose my unique brand of arthritis. She has a very difficult job! Rheumatology deals with all kinds of inflammatory illnesses, such as Lupus and Fibromyalgia as well as countless forms of arthritis.

On a recent visit I asked her, "What's the hardest part of diagnosing someone?" Without much hesitation she said, "Getting all the information." She went on to say that to make the right diagnosis she needed to be able to see the big picture. That requires not just blood tests, but a good idea of exactly what hurts and when it started hurting.

Often when people come to see her they only talk about what is hurting them that day. They neglect to talk about the nagging back pain they've had for the past six months or the soreness in their hips that comes and goes. People have a tendency to focus on the pain they are feeling in the moment. But knowing about the progression of pain in a patient makes a big difference in diagnosis.

Another obstacle to proper diagnosis is people who are 50 but still think their body should do the same things it did at 20. Our parts start to wear out and arthritis sets in, but instead of addressing the new reality that we live in an old body, we take a few extra Advil and try to ignore it. By the time people finally make an appointment to see the doctor they are practically crippled.

When it comes to the epidemic of failed pastoral transitions in the church the same obstacles to diagnosis can be found. People don't take into account all the information and fail to see the big picture. Instead of tracing things back to a root cause, we focus on the immediate discomfort. And we fail to realize that some things have changed. Things that worked well 20 years ago might not be as effective today.

In this chapter we'll look at a few of the biggest obstacles in diagnosing what's going wrong with our current methods of pastoral succession. These are things that we need to be aware of and work through if there is going to be any healing and change.

That's Not the Way We've Always Done It!

Just about every new pastor has heard these seven words: "That's not how we've always done it!" People love consistency. They struggle with change and new ideas and new ways of doing things, especially in the church, and especially in smaller churches.

14

I tried to keep track of how many times I heard this sentiment in my first year, but I lost count. It didn't always come out in those exact words, but the same idea was conveyed though statements like...

"We can't do that."

"That won't work here."

"That's not who we are."

And my personal favorite...

"We tried that once and it failed."

Even when it is painfully obvious that a ministry is dead, it will still limp along for years because it is a tradition. Minor adjustments to the facility or the liturgy are met with opposition. Casting a new vision and helping people see the value of making strategic changes is one of the hardest parts of the pastor's job.

Anyone who has been a pastor for a few years has discovered that to effectively bring about change in the church you have to take your time. It requires making a clear case for why the old thing is out of date and obsolete. You have to walk that fine line of highlighting the weaknesses in an old program without offending the people who started that program and still love it. You have to be able to cast the vision for what something new would look like and how it would work. Changing things in the church is hard work!

In the same way, changing the way that denominations and pastors think when it comes to pastoral transitions is not an easy thing! As I've interviewed different denominational leaders they all understand that the culture of the church is changing and see the growing problem of failed transitions, but many of them are still tied to their traditional systems. Many of them think that better church assessments or a stronger search committee are the solutions.

When I suggested to the denominational heads that it should be the pastor's job to lead through the succession process I heard a lot of, "We can't do that," "We tried that once and it didn't work," which all amounts to the same thing as saying, "That's not how we've always done it!"

For a long time the preferred method of transition involves the outgoing pastor getting out of the way and the board or search committee doing the work of finding a replacement. But that method contains some inherent problems.[6] Denominations, seminaries, churches, and pastors need to recognize that they can't keep doing things the way we've always done them.

I'm not a fan of changing things just for the sake of change. And it doesn't do much good to do away with one method if there isn't something better to take its place. There are some solid reasons why a change is needed. In the next few chapters I will explain why the old way of replacing a pastor is no longer effective, and then in the

---

[6] Those problems will be addressed in chapter 3.

second section I'll cast a vision for what something new might look like.

It's Not My Job!

A close kin to the idea that "it's not the way we've always done it" is the mentality that most pastors have that it just isn't their job to worry about succession, so they don't plan or budget or lead in a way that takes into account their eventual departure. The first sentence in the book *Next* is this simple, yet profound truth: "Every pastor is an interim pastor."[7] Unless we plan on killing the church or being raptured, all of us are merely temporary shepherds entrusted to care for that congregation for a season.

Perhaps the greatest blind spot within the church world today are pastors who don't think that planning for their succession is their job. There will be no proper diagnosis, no long term health, and no real change until every pastor understands their role in the process is not to simply resign and leave.

Making sure that a healthy transition takes place is one of the most important things that leaders do for their organizations. It is not the board's responsibility. It is not the job of the denomination to find a replacement. It is not something that should be left up to a search committee. It is the pastor's job!

---

[7] Vanderbloemen and Bird, 9.

There has been an unspoken rule in the church world that says that pastors should not be involved in choosing or training their replacements. They should just set a retirement date and quietly fade off into the background. Pastors think that the gracious thing to do is to let the church figure out what they want in their next pastor.

But after talking to experienced denominational leaders, reviewing case studies, studying secular succession strategy, and studying the Scriptures, there is no doubt that the pastor must lead through succession. As the leader of the church the influence a pastor exerts as he is leaving will contribute significantly to the future health of that church.

Whether the outgoing pastor is planning a retirement, planning to move to a different church, or planning on sticking around for another 20 years, it is his job as the leader of that church to think about, talk about, and plan for his departure. The board should help, a search committee might be a part of the process, the denomination can help offer advice, but it is his job to take the lead.

I'm not sure who told pastors that it wasn't their responsibility to lead through a transition. I went on the hunt for the origin of this idea. I started by scouring every book on pastoral succession that I could find. None of them offered any reasoning or explanation, but most of them implied that the pastor was to hand things off to the board and then retire graciously. I found a wealth of advice for boards and search committees, but nothing about the pastor's responsibility.

In the book *Mastering Transitions*, which is one volume in the "Mastering Ministry" series published by Multnomah Press in the 1990's, there is advice on hearing God's call to ministry, acclimating to a new church, and handling difficult situations. But there is very little said about how to leave. The author's advice is simply, "let the board lead." "I felt the board was primarily responsible for preparing the church for my departure. I could give guidance and encouragement, but the board needed to take initiative. Soon I wouldn't be around, and they'd have to fend for themselves while searching for a new pastor."[8]

The clear assumption here is that the process of transition is not the pastor's job; but why not? Why shouldn't he be more involved in the process? Why shouldn't he be the one to take the initiative? Why does he have to leave the board to "fend for themselves?" The pastor is looked to for leadership in every other area of the church; why not this one? For the answers to those questions I turned to men who had spent years serving churches.

I interviewed a number of denominational leaders in my search for answers. These were all men who served as a pastor to pastors. They were either former or active pastors themselves. Some of them had worked as seminary professors or seminary presidents. They had

---

[8] Edward B. Bratcher and Robert G. Kemper and Douglas Scott, *Mastering Transitions* (Portland: Multnomah, 1991), 130.

all helped individual churches walk through the process of pastoral transition. These men have been working in the church world for a long time and have a well formed understanding of church culture.

Each one of them affirmed that there was a general assumption in most churches that the pastor should not be involved with the transition. I asked each of them, "Why don't pastors think it is their job to lead the way in the process of succession?" Their answers primarily followed three lines of reasoning.

First, most churches have a set of constitutional guidelines that they operate under. Most church constitutions contain detailed instructions on the formation and duties of a search committee when a pastor leaves. The constitution seems to say that the job of finding a successor is up to a search committee. So pastors leave under the assumption that their job is done.

Second, many pastors don't want to be seen as overly controlling. They don't want to give the impression that they think they are monarchs who will appoint the next person to sit on the throne. No one likes a dictator. So in an effort to exercise humility most pastors stay out of the selection process.

Third, pastors often want to give the church the freedom to go in a different direction. Maybe they are hoping for someone who is a better evangelist, or a better preacher, or a better visionary. By removing himself from the process he is giving the church the ability to make changes in a way that won't be as awkward.

Each of these reasons makes sense. They help to explain why many pastors today don't think that it is their job to lead their churches through the succession process. It's not that they are negligent or uncaring. They are simply doing the most humble thing according to the wisdom of the day.

However, there is a deeper reason why we do things the way we do them, one that goes back a little further. I had to keep digging before I discovered the origin of the idea that the pastor shouldn't be involved in succession planning. Often the leadership structure within the church will mirror the leadership structures in the business or political realms. The Bible doesn't say anything about governing boards, membership rosters, or democratic voting procedures, but those tools have been adopted by the church because they help to create order. There is nothing wrong with borrowing organizational methods from the business world. Most secular businesses have a governing board. The CEO is accountable to the board and it is the board that hires and fires the leader if the company starts to veer off course. It was not uncommon for businesses to headhunt to find the most talented leader. A good leader was seen as someone who had the right level of education and experience.

These business practices eventually migrated into the church. After all most church boards are made up of men who have been successful in some aspect of business. The church adopted the idea that the board is in charge and oversees hiring and firing of pastors. If a position is open they will go out and look for the best available

21

candidate. A good pastor is someone who has the right level of education and experience.

This secular business model soon became the regular practice in most churches. Seminaries did their job of educating future pastors. Denominations did their job of funneling men into open positions. And the people in the church held in high regard pastoral candidates who had education and experience. New church leaders already had a good measure of respect given to them simply by virtue of their degrees and past accomplishments.

It wasn't hard for a church board to gather a pile of resumes and select the right man for the job, or in some cases go out and headhunt a pastor who seemed to be doing well at another church. The secular business method for choosing new leaders has served the church somewhat well in the past.

However, culture changes. The business world is far better at identifying the changes and adapting. So when cultural shifts take place they can adjust in a matter of years, but it often takes the church decades to make the same kind of adjustments. Sometimes by the time we realize that culture has shifted and we need to adjust, it has shifted again. The church seems to always be lagging behind.

Pastors and churches adopted a secular management strategy because it was familiar and it got the job done. It has become such an ingrained part of church methodology for so long that it has started to feel like a biblical mandate. But the idea that the pastor should not be involved in the succession process is not found anywhere in the Bible!

It seems the idea that it isn't the pastor's job to equip and train his replacement is a leftover from an old secular business strategy that crept into the church. Ironically, that methodology has largely been abandoned in the business world. The secular world has already made the shift to something different in response to cultural changes.

The bestselling book, *The Leadership Pipeline*, represents a newer method of succession planning that requires more training, more involvement from the current leader, and intentional preparation for the inevitable change in leadership. The authors define succession planning in this way: "Succession planning is perpetuating the enterprise by filling the pipeline with high-performing people to ensure that every leadership level has an abundance of these performers to draw from, both now and in the future."[9] It's increasingly more common to find companies that train their own people and hire from within. However, in the church we are still sifting through stacks of resumes and hiring outsiders.

I'm not advocating that the church simply adopt the secular strategy of the day. However, the business world can help us better understand our culture and give us valuable insight into practices that are no longer as effective. As the world we live in changes, our approach to church management should adapt accordingly.

---

[9] Ram Charan, Steve Drotter, Jim Noel, *The Leadership Pipeline: How to Build the Leadership Powered Company* (San Francisco: Jossey-Bass, 2011), 207.

Even though succession planning wasn't the pastor's job in the past, there are some compelling reasons to believe that it should be in the future. We will investigate some of these reasons in the next section.

Failure to Adapt to Cultural Changes

Everything changes. Sometimes the changes are rapid, and sometimes the changes are barely noticeable. Hairstyles change, church attendance patterns change, acceptable worship attire changes, communities change, and music styles change. A huge obstacle in our ability to properly diagnose and treat the problem of failed transitions is due to the fact that we have failed to recognize and adapt to some significant cultural shifts.

The main reason that it takes the church so long to make changes is because we hold tradition and consistency in high regard. But sometimes there is confusion about which things are immovable biblical mandates and which things are merely preferences or modern methods. Sometimes we can even begin to think the color of the carpet or the placement of the piano bench is divinely inspired.

Another reason it takes the church so long to adjust is because the societal changes are often very subtle. The shifts are easy for us to miss if we aren't looking. There are plenty of businesses that also miss the cues and find themselves in trouble. But the ones that survive and thrive are usually good at understanding the culture around them.

I have identified five of the most significant cultural shifts that have taken place in recent years. These things have already affected the church in different ways. There are no doubt others that we could add to the list, but these five things directly affect succession planning within the church.

Relational Over Professional

There's an old adage that says people don't care how much you know until they know how much you care. People value your heart more than your brain. Perhaps this sentiment is truer today than it was 50 years ago.

There was a time when certain occupations carried with them a high degree of respect. Politicians, doctors, public servants, and preachers were honored because of their title and position in the community. People with a certain level of education were respected simply because of the degree they had earned and the profession they had chosen.

But today educational achievement doesn't seem to matter to people nearly as much as relational concern. There has been a shift from placing a high priority on Intelligence Quotient (IQ) to placing a higher priority on Emotional Quotient (EQ). In a recent *Forbes* article Steve Cooper explains why employees with a high EQ are more effective than those with a high IQ. Mr. Cooper shares a study that revealed "emotional intelligence was a better predictor of success than either relevant previous experience or high IQ."[10]

That reality has some significant implications for the church. The majority of our search committees still believe that a minimum of 5 years of experience and a Master's degree are the most important standards for the new pastor. Our current methods of succession are not very well suited to measure EQ.

We want doctors who will take the time to listen to us, and it's a bonus if they are also really good at medicine. Dignity Health, a corporation that runs hospitals in California, has as their motto, "Hello Humankindness". The emphasis isn't that they have the most educated and well trained doctors available, but that they will be nice to you when you come visit them.

There is a very real shift that has taken place. There was a time when professional ability was preferred over friendliness. What mattered most was that a person had the right education and experience. It didn't matter how much they cared, it mattered what they knew. But today we are just fine with someone with a lower level of professional ability if they have higher relational abilities.

---

[10] Steve Cooper, "Look For Employees with High EQ Over IQ" *Forbes.com,* <http://www.forbes.com/sites/stevecooper/2013/03/18/look-for-employees-with-high-eq-over-iq/> (Accessed June 10, 2015)

This kind of cultural shift is subtle. It's hard to quantify and easy to overlook. There aren't a lot of studies or surveys that help those of us within the church to spot the change. Friendliness has always been a good thing and professional competency is still needed, but today the ability to connect with other people is absolutely essential.

I asked my panel of denominational leaders, "Do you think that there has been a shift in our culture away from professionalism in leadership and towards leaders who are more relational?" Without exception they all agreed.

A number of them talked about how most search committees seem to still be focused on professional abilities. The search committee gets so focused on their printed guidelines that they pass over a loving, caring man in favor of the minister with the extra degree. But the members of the congregation really just want to know that their pastor loves them. Pastoral failures are rarely due to theological disagreement or moral failure, but ultimately due to the pastor's inability to connect with the people.

There was a time when a Master of Divinity (M.Div.) degree was required if someone wanted to be a senior pastor. It was fine for an associate or youth pastor to just have a Bachelor's degree, but the senior pastor had to have more than that. There are some churches that still have this requirement written into their constitution.

At my alma mater, and in many other seminaries across the country, there has been a significant drop in M.Div. enrollment.

There are undoubtedly a number of factors that contribute to this trend: the economy, increased undergraduate costs, and an increase in specialized degrees might be some of those factors. But perhaps another reason is that in most churches the congregation, and even the board, has no idea what the difference is between M.Div. and M.A. degrees.

The average church member today is just not that impressed by a pastor's level of education. They want a pastor who is personable and friendly and can communicate the Bible in an understandable way. Education is not a bad thing; it's just not the main thing anymore.

This kind of shift toward pastors who are more warm and relational calls for some changes in the way we train and choose pastors. Using constitutional guidelines written in the 1950's that screen for the most educated man will lead to unnecessary frustration and failure. Today the right fit needs to be someone who knows and loves the community and the congregation. That takes a lot more time to find or train.

Insider Over Outsider

In the bestselling book, *Good to Great*, Jim Collins set out to discover what makes some businesses great, while others flounder or even fail. Mr. Collins identifies a number of important leadership and institutional factors that seem to always be present in companies that move from being merely good to truly great. He highlights eleven businesses that made the jump from good to great.

Mr. Collins discovered, "Ten of eleven good-to-great CEOs came from *inside* the company, three of them by family inheritance. The comparison companies turned to outsiders with *six times* greater frequency - yet they failed to produce sustained great results."[11] His findings suggest that there is greater stability and success with an insider.

The secular business world has discovered that hiring an insider is significantly better than hiring an outsider. Because people value relationship over professionalism the leader who already knows the culture and customs of the company will have a greater likelihood of succeeding. The most successful companies have discovered that training and hiring from within leads to more effective leadership transitions.

A 2012 study of employment trends showed that it was better to hire from within rather than from outside the company. "Not only were outside hires more expensive, but they were also 61% more likely to be laid off or fired from that position and 21% more likely than internal hires in similar positions to leave a job on their own accord." [12]

[11] James C. Collins, *Good to Great: Why Some Companies Make the Leap--and Others Don't* (New York, NY: Harper Business, 2001), 32.

In 2011 James Sinegal, the co-founder and CEO of Costco, stepped down from his place of leadership. He was 75-years-old at the time and ready to hand things off to the next leader. The replacement was a man named Craig Jelinek who had been working for Costco since 1984. Jelinek was someone who clearly understood the culture and operating principles of Costco and was committed to maintaining them. He had been intentionally groomed to take over the leadership responsibilities from Sinegal.

Costco is a perfect example of a company that recognizes much of its success comes from its culture and values. It's not just a faceless corporation. The people who work at Costco and the people who shop at Costco care about that culture. Failure to maintain it would inevitably lead to disaster.[13]

The need to preserve values, carry on the vision, and maintain the culture is even more important in the church. However, too many churches don't realize the importance of hiring from within. Many churches are clueless as to how to train and groom a leader from within. Hiring from the outside leaves a new pastor with the increasingly difficult task of having to learn and acclimate to a new culture before they can ever implement any change.

---

[12] Melissa Korn, "Is It Better to Promote From Within?" *Wall Street Journal* http://www.wsj.com/articles/SB1000142405270230475040457732000004103550 4> (Accessed July 10, 2015)

[13] Ann Zimmerman, "Costco CEO to Step Down," *Wall Street Journal* <http://www.wsj.com/articles/SB1000142405311190389590457654488839647210 42> (Accessed June 10, 2015)

An insider with the right heart seems to be more successful than an outsider with a lot of credentials. That might not have always been true, but it is today. The most successful secular businesses have adapted to this reality. It's time for the church to catch up.

In *The Leadership Baton* this cultural shift is noted:

In the past, many church leaders who wanted to do ministry better hired the most extraordinary people they could find to come in and make their churches beautiful. This was an expensive and often very difficult process. Today more and more churches are looking to their native soil, where they find people who have proven in earlier ministry roles their character, their fit with the church's culture, and their faithfulness. These churches see such choices as not just the safest ones but also the best ones.[14]

The most successful pastoral transitions will take place when the new pastor is brought up from within the church. However, in most of our churches we do not have any pipeline established to identify, train, and equip new pastors. We are left searching for an outsider because not enough time and thought is given to ways we might bring up an insider. That has to change!

---

[14] Rowland Forman and Jeff Jones and Bruce Miller, *The Leadership Baton: An Intentional Strategy for Developing Leaders in Your Church* (Grand Rapids, MI: Zondervan, 2004), 38.

Independence Over Denominationalism

In past decades denominations were an important part of the pastoral succession process. The denomination served as a point of connection between men who were looking for a church and churches that were looking for their next pastor. The denomination would ordain and recommend potential candidates. There was a closer relationship between the head of the denomination and the church.

In the past twenty years many churches have been removing denominational labels from their name in an effort to be more welcoming to people seeking a church home. This has led to a devaluing of denominational affiliation. The rise of nondenominational church planting organizations such as Acts 29 has also contributed to the shift towards independence. Churches are less likely to be a part of a denomination or seek help from their denomination.

In a *Christianity Today* article from June of 2015 Ed Stetzer shares his take on statistics that show a sharp increase in non-denominationalism in America. Most new church plants are choosing to remain unaffiliated or collaborate with many different denominations. And most individuals no longer self-identify with a particular denomination. Pastor Stetzer shows that, "over the last four decades, there has been more than a 400 percent growth in Protestants who identify as nondenominational."[15]

As I interviewed various denominational leaders from different parts of the country they indicated that fewer and fewer churches are coming to them for help with a transition. Many of the churches they do work with are the ones that are unhealthy and struggling. Two separate regional directors used the word "triage" to describe their involvement with most churches. The denomination is only called in when things are a mess and hanging by a thread.

As a pastor who is a part of a Baptist association, I see the value of denominational affiliation. I also recognize that the role of the denomination is changing. In the past denominations were very helpful with the placement process. In the future the greatest value from the denomination will be to educate pastors on how to train and develop the next leader. As the church becomes more independent we will need to get better at developing our own leaders who can carry on the work of ministry.

Specialized Over General

The fast food giant McDonald's started a financial slide in 2014 and has continually seen a drop in revenue every quarter in 2015. There have been a number of articles written to try and diagnose the problem. An article by reporter Cassie Shortsleeve blames the drop in sales on the fact that Millennials want to know what is in their

[15] Ed Stetzer, "The Rapid Rise of Nondenominational Christianity" *Christianity Today* http://www.christianitytoday.com/edstetzer/2015/june/rapid-rise-of-non-denominational-christianity-my-most-recen.html (Accessed February 3, 2016)

food. This new generation places a higher value on authenticity and transparency. They are drawn to trendy small places that appear to have fresher ingredients.[16]

There are some lessons that the church can learn from what's happening at McDonald's. The reason we like eating at a chain restaurant is because we know what to expect. McDonald's is going to have pretty much the same menu and the same quality of food no matter where you go. The church used to operate more like a chain restaurant.

There was a day when you knew what to expect with a Baptist church, a Presbyterian church, or a Lutheran church. Whether you were in California or Minnesota, they all had a similar theological menu, the same basic liturgy, and identical ministries. But today each church is more like a boutique than a chain.

Instead of carbon copy ministries, we've realized that we can do things that are more relevant to our communities. Each church often has a specialty: recovery ministry, college ministry, family ministry, etc. Many churches have adopted the "Hedgehog Principle" found in *Good to Great* of doing one thing well instead of doing lots of things poorly.[17] The mission might be the same from church to church, but the way that mission is accomplished varies greatly.

---

[16] Cassie Shortsleeve, "Why Millennials Just Aren't That Into McDonald's," *Yahoo.com,* https://www.yahoo.com/health/why-millennials-just-arent-that-into-mcdonalds-126035358772.html (August 20, 2015)

[17] Colins, 118-119

Fifty years ago, when churches were more like chain restaurants, they could choose a candidate that had the standard education and experience. But today the best candidate will be the man who understands the culture of the church and the unique impact the church has in its particular community. It's becoming increasingly important to have a pastor who is a specialist and not a generalist.

High Mobility Over Low Mobility

Another significant cultural shift affecting the way we do leadership succession is our society's incredible mobility. Long gone are the days of working at the same place for 40 years. One study shows that the average work tenure today is 4.4 years and falling.[18]

The side effect of a transient work force means that people do not settle down and live in the same house or community for 40+ years anymore. That means much higher turnover rates within the church as some people move out and new people move in.

---

[18] Anya Kamenetz, "The Four-Year Career," *Fastcompany.com*, http://www.fastcompany.com/1802731/four-year-career (Accessed December 12,2015)

Grandpa and Grandma both had the same jobs, the same house, and the same church for their whole lives. They weathered through the good times and the bad. They were far more likely to stand by their company and their community and their church. If a new pastor was hired who wasn't a good fit they would simply wait him out. Today people will bolt to the church down the street at the first sign of discomfort.

This new reality is just one of the reasons that the process of leadership transition has become increasingly traumatic to many churches. The honeymoon period is a lot shorter and the need for a smooth handoff is even greater.

At many secular companies the discussion about succession planning happens as soon as a new leader is hired. The understanding is that there is a great likelihood their CEO won't be there for the next 40 years. If turnover at the highest levels of leadership is happening more frequently, then they have to get really good at replacing those leaders.[19]

A high turnover rate in leadership isn't a good thing for businesses or churches. The sweet spot in ministry often doesn't happen until about year five or six.[20] In the church, consistency is

---

[19] Jena McGregor, "The Rate of CEO Change," Washingtonpost.com, <https://www.washingtonpost.com/national/on-leadership/the-rate-of-ceo-turnover/2012/05/24/gJQAJrAMnU_story.html> (Accessed June 24, 2015).

[20]Charles Arn, "Pastoral Longevity and Church Growth," *Wesleyconnectonline.com*, <http://wesleyconnectonline.com/pastoral-longevity-and-church-growth-charles-arn/> (June 10, 2015).

always an asset. But there's a good likelihood that the pulpit will not be immune from the cultural shift towards higher mobility.

If shorter pastoral tenures and a higher turnover rates are in our future, then churches will have to get better at identifying, training, and transitioning in new leaders.

These are just a few of the ways that our culture has changed in the past few decades. These shifts have led to increasing frustration and failure as the church tries to use the same old succession playbook. Hiring an outsider who doesn't understand the culture or context of a particular church may lead to disaster.

The Elephant in the Board Room saw this culture shift taking place over a decade ago:

> Unfortunately, we often operate out of a church paradigm that worked fifty years ago. In that era of high denominational loyalty, transitions were much less disorienting owing to off-the-shelf ministry approaches universally applied, simple programmatic paths to success (worship, Sunday school, youth group), an ample supply of ministers, and low mobility among church members. People tended to stay with a church through its transition, and the new pastor from Seattle used the same curriculum as the former pastor from Bloomington.

Today, ministry is much more localized, customized, specialized, and complex.[21]

Things have changed. The pastor who loves his church must not leave succession planning up to the board or a search committee. He must recognize that healthy succession is a key part of his job as the leader of the church.

---

[21] Carolyn Weese and J. Russell Crabtree, *The Elephant in the Boardroom: Speaking the Unspoken about Pastoral Transitions* (San Francisco, CA: Jossey-Bass, 2004), 5.

Chapter 3

THE ROOT CAUSE

Treating symptoms instead of the root cause is a waste of time. It doesn't really lead to long-term health. Just focusing on the symptoms might numb the pain a little, but in the end it only makes things worse. When it comes to the problem with pastoral transitions the root cause is not faulty search committees, or lots of bad replacement pastors, or a congregational fear of change; those things are secondary issues. The root cause can be traced back to a simple lack in pastoral leadership.

God has given pastors the responsibility to equip, train, guide, and protect the church. When a church is ingrown and disconnected from the community, the root cause is often a leader who has failed to properly communicate the mission of the church. When a church freaks out over minor changes, often the root cause is a pastor who has failed to patiently lead people through the process. When a congregation has a crumbling moral foundation, it's usually caused by a failure to lead people to greater holiness and devotion to Christ. And when a church shrivels in the years following a change of pastor, the root cause can often be traced back to a leader who failed to plan and prepare for his departure.

When a pastor does not think that it is his job to plan for his departure it creates a leadership void within the church. In this chapter I want to encourage pastors to see themselves as the leader of their church. There are some obstacles that can often make it difficult for a pastor to be the leader that God has called him to be. Before he can take the lead in the process of succession, he must first take up the mantle of leadership.

The Pastoral Leadership Void

Many pastors have a weird understanding of leadership. Even with the multitude of books on leadership that line our shelves, we still often don't see ourselves as the leader. There are too many churches that have a pastor, but not a leader. What follows are some common reasons why pastors struggle to truly lead.

Church Government Structures

In some cases the church structure makes it hard for the pastor to be a leader. A church with a strong congregational polity or a heavily involved board doesn't want the pastor to be a leader, but to be a hireling who will do the preaching and visitations.

Churches that have been hurt by an overbearing pastor in the past are more likely to protect themselves by taking authority away from the pastoral position and shifting it to the board. The pastor is treated with suspicion and not allowed to make any real changes in the church. This tendency is understandable, but not at all biblical or healthy.

In some churches the pastor is not a voting member of the board and has a very limited amount of power. The board makes the big decisions and actively works to keep the pastor in a subordinate place. The problem is that people don't follow boards, they follow leaders. The pastor will still be seen as the leader. Even if the church structure has the pastor somewhere near the bottom of the organizational chart, the people in the church will still view him as the boss. He has to find a way to patiently, humbly, lovingly lead within that kind of context even though it will be more challenging.

Poor Leadership Training

The bulk of theological training that pastors undergo is focused on how to study and communicate God's word. Seminary prepares us well for our role as resident theologian or preacher, but there are few leadership courses. We enter the ministry not really knowing how to cast a vision or manage a board or lead through change.

In a study conducted in 2006 by the Francis A. Schaeffer Institute of Church Leadership Development 75% of pastors said they felt unqualified and poorly trained to lead and manage the church.[22] There are so many demands made on a pastor that we can often feel overwhelmed and inadequate.

The denominational leaders that I interviewed recognize this lack of leadership training and have taken steps to offer assessment and education to pastors in their region. One of the benefits of being a part of a particular denomination is the ongoing support that they provide. However, many pastors just don't take advantage of the resources that are available.

Many pastors think that leadership ability will come with time and experience. That might be true to a certain extent but, just like any skill, the ability to lead won't grow without some training. He might become a little better preacher over time, but real development in his ability to communicate the word of God takes an intentional investment. It might involve reading books on preaching, going to preaching seminars, and listening to pastors who are really good preachers. In the same way, leadership development will require intentional study. It will take reading books on leadership and going to leadership conferences and being around really good leaders.

Pastoral training doesn't end after seminary. Seek out opportunities to develop greater knowledge and skill in this area.

Dictator Fear

---

[22] Dr. Richard J. Krejcir "Statistics on Pastors" *Into the Word* http://www.intothyword.org/apps/articles/?articleid=36562(Accessed June 4,2015)

No pastor wants to be viewed as a dictator. We've all seen ugly examples of men who have used the church as a means of personal gain and we don't want to be accused of that ourselves. If we exert too much authority people will be offended, but if we don't take on any responsibility we aren't truly leaders. We need to stop being afraid of being strong, loving leaders.

I appreciate the desire not to be seen as domineering and controlling, but don't swing to the opposite extreme where you pass off every decision and allow others to take the church in the wrong direction. There are some things that are worth fighting for. Be a strong leader who continually upholds the Great Commission. Be a leader who doesn't allow any worthless thing to distract people. Be a leader who defends the truth of Scripture. Be a leader who looks out for the health and future of the church!

In the book *Sticky Teams* Larry Osborne offers some great advice to pastors on how to guard against becoming a dictator. "1. Present first drafts, no final proposals; 2. Keep no secrets from the board; 3. Follow the board's advice."[23] The board that God has put around you can help keep you accountable. A healthy board will empower the pastor to be the kind of leader that God has called him to be.

Manager Syndrome

---

[23] Larry Osborne, *Sticky Teams* (Grand Rapids: Zondervan, 2010), 95.

Warren Bennis wrote a number of books on leadership development. In many of his books he explains the difference between leaders and managers. In *Why Leaders Can't Lead* Bennis says, "Most organizations are underled and overmanaged."[24] This reality can be found in the church.

There is a real difference between what a leader does and what a manager does. Bennis offers this list:

– The manager administers; the leader innovates.

– The manager maintains; the leader develops.

– The manager focuses on systems and structure; the leader focuses on people.

– The manager relies on control; the leader inspires trust.

– The manager has a short-range view; the leader has a long-range perspective.

– The manager asks how and when; the leader asks what and why.

– The manager has his or her eye always on the bottom line; the leader's eye is on the horizon.

– The manager imitates; the leader originates.

---

[24] Warren Bennis, *Why Leaders Can't Lead: The Unconscious Conspiracy Continues* (San Francisco: Jossey-Bass, 1989), 18.

– The manager accepts the status quo; the leader challenges it.

– The manager is the classic good soldier; the leader is his or her own person.

– The manager does things right; the leader does the right thing. [25]

Every church needs managers: those people who can spend time with the details, maintain healthy systems, and paint within the lines. Managers don't care about the big picture. They don't need to know how all the parts fit together. They are content to focus on their area of ministry. Managers are essential in every healthy church.

But many pastors get stuck managing details and never rise to the level of leader. Pastors are notoriously bad at delegation and end up wading into the weeds in too many areas of church life. They are on every committee, managing the budget, fixing the toilets, raking the leaves. There's no time for big picture leadership.

The danger of managing instead of leading is far greater for pastors of smaller churches. In a church of 500 or more it becomes too difficult to manage every detail. Pastors are required to delegate and trust others to manage systems. But small church pastors are often expected to do every single ministry job at the church. Considering that 94% of the churches in America are under 500

---

[25] Bennis, 18.

people, that means an awful lot of pastors are stuck managing more than leading.

Even the smallest church needs leadership. Every church needs someone who is thinking ahead and developing new ways of reaching people, and making healthy changes to those old systems. Every church needs a leader who is more concerned with the church as a whole, and not just the bottom line.

Pastors fail to rise above the level of manager to the level of leader because it is hard. It requires a clear understanding of our gifting, a good evaluation of the gifts of others, and the courage to question the status quo. Take some time to evaluate yourself and pray about ways you can transition from being a church manager to a leader.

The pastor is called to be more than just the preacher, the theologian, or the errand boy; he is called to be the leader. The reason for much of the trauma in churches at the point of transition is a significant lack of leadership. I truly believe that if every pastor understood his biblical role as the leader of the church then the problem with pastoral transitions would be solved.

It wasn't until my fifth year in ministry that I began to see myself as the leader. I took a class from Pastor Larry Osborne. Through his teaching and through his book, *Sticky Teams*, he encouraged me to be a leader.[26] He showed me from God's word that God expects me

---

[26] Osborne, 87-100.

to be the leader of my church, not just an employee. Pastor Osborne explains, "Research has consistently shown that strong pastoral leadership is a key ingredient in virtually every healthy and growing church."[27] Those are sobering and convicting words. For the sake of the church pastors must be willing to take the lead.

Pastor, I want to encourage you to take up the reigns of leadership in your church. Lead with humility and love, but lead! Lead as one who will give an account, but lead! Lead through the rough times and through the successes. Lead through the power of the Holy Spirit, not your own power. Lead as one who deeply loves the body of Christ!

The Succession Leadership Void

This is a book about healthy leadership. It's not really about how to leave well; it's more about how to lead well. This isn't a retirement manual for pastors on their way out, but a call to stand and lead for those who are still in the thick of things. Healthy transitions happen when a church has a healthy leader who understands that it is his job to lead all the way to the very end, and then even beyond.

Most pastors are sacrificially serving their church. Pastors feel the weight of their calling every single day. And we know that

---

[27] Osborne, 100.

without the help of the Holy Spirit there is no way we can do anything. Pastors work hard to preach the word of God with excellence. They strive to cast vision and lead people to do new things. They manage the resources of the church faithfully. They recognize that they have been entrusted with something that is very important to God.

The reason that many pastors fail to take responsibility to lead through a transition is not because they are lazy or apathetic. It's not due to a lack of love for their church. Every pastor wants to see their church thrive once they are gone. So why do so few pastors see the transition process as a part of their leadership responsibilities?

I Don't Have Time for Succession Planning

First, all of the other leadership responsibilities on the pastor's plate are way more pressing. People are looking to him every single day to teach, preach, cast vision, disciple, and manage resources. Failure to lead well in one of these areas will be noticed right away. But my guess is no one is asking if he has a solid succession plan in place.

There are blogs written every day urging pastors to do a better job of welcoming new people into their church or managing staff or avoiding ministry silos, but there are not too many blogs about how to identify and train a successor. We are way too busy dealing with the worries of today to think much about tomorrow.

In the book *Seamless Succession* Dr. Passavant explains how being proactive is generally healthier than being reactive when it comes to succession planning.

We spend far more time reacting to situations than we do proactively creating a healthy culture that lends itself to producing new ideas, developing leaders, and being receptive to change. What can happen as a result of this approach, especially in a succession event, is that things can - and will - quickly spiral out of control, causing us to spend months unnecessarily scrambling due to lack of preparation.[28]

For a busy pastor finding the time to invest in succession planning is not easy. There are just too many other needs that are more urgent.

I Didn't Know I was Supposed to Do Succession Planning

Second, no one told us it was our job. It's not in the job description. It isn't something that is talked about until a resignation or retirement is imminent. Some pastors don't think it is their job, but most just don't think about it at all.

Vanderbloemen and Bird point out, "It seems odd that so many pastors give strong leadership in many strategic areas but stop

---

[28] Dr. Jay Passavant, *Seamless Succession: Simplifying Church Leadership* (Xulon Press, 2015) 55.

leading when it comes to succession issues. Why? We think it's because there are so few models. It's just not the norm - yet!"[29] Pastors fail to lead in this area simply because they don't see other pastors doing it.

Very few of the different denominational leaders I interviewed were instructing pastors on how to plan and prepare for their successor. Many of them didn't think that the pastor should be a part of the process. These denominational leaders had seen too many examples of pastors who did a lousy job of exiting and were left with the general assumption that, if it was left to the pastor, he'd just screw it up. They referred to pastors as "not very strategic," "not self-aware," and "not able to develop leaders."

I know there will always be pastors who aren't great leaders, but the idea that most pastors can't or shouldn't lead their church through the process of succession is absurd. It's like saying that most pastors can't effect positive change in their church, or proclaim the Great Commission, or influence people to deeper spiritual growth, or shepherd through tragedy. A pastor is called to be a leader! They can and do lead well in dozens of different ways.

I might be biased because I am a pastor, but I think that there are a lot of really good pastors who lead well and have a lot to offer their church as they navigate the transition process. There's no doubt that this has been an area of weakness for many senior pastors in the past,

---

[29] Vanderbloemen and Bird, 27.

but this is a skill that we need to learn moving forward. Each denominational leader that I interviewed was doing a great job of helping to equip pastors to be better leaders in the areas of preaching and counseling and administration. It's time that they add a yearly workshop for pastors on how to plan for their departure.

When I talk to fellow pastors and tell them that it is their job to think about succession I can see the light go on in their heads. It's clear that for many of them they have just never been told that it is their responsibility. It's amazing to see how their natural leadership abilities kick in and they start to brainstorm solutions and think about possible strategies. All they needed was to be encouraged to take the lead in that area.

Succession Planning is Too Risky

Third, sometimes pastors fail to plan for their departure simply because thinking about leaving is hard. There are some significant risks involved with the process of succession planning. We know that it is inevitable, but we hope to ignore that reality for as long as we can. But burying our head in the sand doesn't make our departure any easier; it only makes our church more unstable.

The Elephant in the Board Room asks the question, "When it comes to pastoral transition, leaders often stop leading. Why? The reasons for silence seem to be rooted more in fear and low self-confidence."[30] The whole conversation is just too scary.

51

Succession planning carries with it the risk of discovering that the board, and maybe even the church, is looking forward to the pastor's departure. I believe that some pastors intentionally refuse to talk about retirement or resignation for fear that once they start talking about it people will force them out. It is way easier to just ignore the whole conversation.

Creating a leadership pipeline and mentoring future leaders is also a risk of time and money. It's possible that a pastor could invest in hiring and training a man to take over for him, only to have that man move to a different church or decide not to step into leadership. There are no guarantees that the man he grooms for the pastoral role will work out.

Then there is the risk that people in the church might like the protégé more than they like the pastor. No pastor would admit it out loud, but the idea of bringing in someone younger and hipper who might turn out to be a better preacher is horrifying! That deep insecurity creates a barrier that keeps him from investing in others. He can easily claim that he doesn't have the time or the money, but the real reason is often a desire to remain the star.

I'm Afraid of Losing Control

---

[30] Weese <u>and</u> Crabtree, 14.

Finally, pastors often avoid the process of succession planning because of a fear of losing control. Pastors often struggle to delegate small tasks to other people in the church. It can be even more frightening to delegate big things. We want to stay in control of when we leave and how we leave. We want to shape our own future. Succession planning might force us into a situation that we aren't in control of anymore.

I recognize that what I am asking pastors to do is something very difficult. Asking them to shed an old way of thinking is hard enough, but asking men to take part in a process that will eventually result in being jobless is frightening. Pastors must get past this fear for the greater good of the church.

There is a very real and understandable fear that pastors face when they think about leaving. Vanderbloemen and Bird point out, "Perhaps no career ties identity to job more than the pastorate. What other job coincides with more key parts of life? Who else performs their daughter's wedding at work? Who else buries longtime friends as a part of their job? What other career ties personal spiritual formation to career performance?"[31]

Again, my goal in writing this book is primarily to encourage and empower pastors to see succession planning as an important part of their job. Whoever told them that is wasn't their job was wrong. I know this isn't the most pressing leadership responsibility, but

---

[31] Vanderbloemen and Bird, 41.

53

failure here will be just as destructive as the mismanagement of funds or a failure to disciple people. For the sake of the health of the church pastors must begin to see succession planning as their God-ordained responsibility!

The Leadership Void Created by the Search Committee

G.K. Chesterton quipped, "I've searched all the parks in all the cities and found no statues of committees." The point he was making is that committees don't really lead. That's not their purpose. The strength of a committee is found in its ability to gather people together to accomplish particular tasks, to manage resources, and to evaluate systems, but committees are not a suitable replacement for leadership.

Pastor Mark Dever views the search committee as a failure of the pastor and church board to adequately prepare for a transition. He sees the search committee as a poor last resort. He says, "This is like making the teenage son and daughter parent their younger siblings because mom and dad are absent. The teenagers can get the job done, and how grateful we are for them. But they inevitably do the work with a limp because they lack the natural resources and advantages of the parents."[32]

---

[32] Mark Dever, "What's Wrong With Search Committees?" *9Marks.com* http://9marks.org/article/whats-wrong-search-committees-part-1-2-finding-pastor/ (Accessed February 4, 2016)

An event as important and delicate as a change of the senior pastor requires careful, strategic, intentional leadership, not a committee. Every denominational leader that I interviewed and every book on pastoral transitions that I read had something to say about the weaknesses of search committees. They all offered advice on how to overcome some of those weaknesses and build a better committee, but even the best run search committee is still just a committee. It lacks some of the essential leadership qualities that are necessary for a healthy transition.

Search Committees Lack Perspective

Pastors with a church that operates with a board structure of any kind will feel the frustration that comes from dealing with board members who are clueless about what the pastor does all week long. It's so hard to try and explain what the ministry is really like. He can give them his office hours, explain how long it takes to write a sermon, and talk about how often he goes on visitations, but that doesn't capture the whole picture.

It's tough to express to a group of businessmen what it's like to be on call 24/7. It's hard for them to understand the weight that's felt with every counseling session and Bible lesson. They don't get what it's like to have every single family vacation interrupted by a sudden death or emergency issue. They often just look at individual ministries without really knowing the big picture of staff issues, volunteer struggles, and personality conflicts.

No one knows the heart and soul of the church better than its pastor. Just like the great Shepherd knows His sheep, a good under shepherd knows his sheep. Because of the work that God has called pastors to do, they have insight into the church that is absolutely unique.

That doesn't mean that other people don't know what's going on, don't love the church, or lack any insight. Hopefully the men on the board have deep love for the church and a desire to understand things in a way that enables them to make wise decisions. But that board rotates every few years and those men have their own full-time jobs, and things change over time. Often the only constant is the pastor.

Most search committees are ether run by the board or a sub-committee of the board. They simply do not possess the same kind of insight about the church that the senior pastor does. They end up painting a skewed picture of the church that reflects only their limited experiences. They often search for someone who will meet their own felt needs, and they have no way of accurately passing information on to the candidates.

One of the most common accusations made by struggling new pastors is that the search committee was dishonest. Lifeway Research found that 48% of pastors felt that the search committee did not accurately describe the church before they arrived.[33] New pastors use the things communicated by the committee during the hiring process to justify changes in the church, and are surprised when the people in the church start to grumble.

I don't think any search committee has ever set out to be intentionally misleading. They offer to the candidate their honest perspective and desire for the church. The particular people on the search committee might genuinely want the church to become more contemporary and believe with all their hearts that livelier music will be a good thing for the church. But that doesn't mean the rest of the church feels the same way.

The new pastor arrives excited to change things and freshen the place up, only to get a load of hate mail within his first month. The search committee wasn't lying; they simply didn't see the big picture. The committee lacked the perspective to be able to communicate how and when change should take place. They weren't able to point out all the possible obstacles to change.

Search committees can't pass on perspective and insight to potential candidates because they just don't have it to give. Their ability to give advice and direction is limited. They haven't been the ones visiting people in the hospital, counseling couples through rough patches, and helping to pray with those who are hurting. The

---

[33] Lisa Cannon Green, "Former Pastors Report Lack of Support Led to Abandoning Pastorate" *Lifeway research* <http://www.lifewayresearch.com/2016/01/12/former-pastors-report-lack-of-support-led-to-abandoning-pastorate/> (Accessed January 12, 2016)

search committee doesn't know the heart and soul of the congregation like a pastor does.

This is a very real problem. My panel of denominational experts all commented on the limitations inherent in the search committee. They have seen dozens of search committees make huge hiring errors simply because they lacked perspective. The solution was to encourage every church to undergo an assessment by an outside agency. The idea is that an outside group can do a better job of identifying the strengths and weaknesses of the church and determining what kind of pastor would be the best fit.

I'm a huge fan of outside assessment and believe that just about every church could benefit from the process, but assessment alone can't solve all of the problems with the search committee. The assessment might offer a little better insight, but it can't provide leadership.

Search Committees Lack Theological Balance

Search committees don't understand the theology of the church. Most committees are unable to ask the right theological questions, or have a very narrow and particular theology that doesn't necessarily reflect the church as a whole.

In my two case studies, the search committee at FBC happened to have a number of very Calvinistic leaning men. The rest of the church didn't share that theological perspective; in fact, most of them were more closely aligned with Arminian ideas. The Calvinistic search committee leaned heavily towards a pastor who was a strong proponent of that theological system.

The new pastor came with the understanding that it was a Calvinistic church that was looking for strong Calvinistic teaching. It's not at all surprising that he lasted less than two years. He felt like he had been lied to. The problem was that he only saw the theology of the people on the committee and didn't discover the true theological makeup of the church until he started preaching.

Every church is unique and nuanced in its theological makeup. Even though each church has a printed set of doctrinal beliefs, the way those doctrines work from one church to the next is very different. Even within the same denomination there can be a difference in emphasis and priority that shapes how we understand and apply different doctrines. Different pastors, different levels of education, different theological interests, different cultural trends, and different ministry needs result in no two churches having exactly the same theology.

It all goes back to perspective. A pastor who has served his church for a number of years understands that the theology of the church is much more complicated than the doctrinal statements in the search committee's packet. The old pastor is keenly aware of the big group of people who migrated over from the Presbyterian

Church a few years ago. He understands that most people are dispensational in the church, but not in a classic way. He knows that youth ministry is a sacred cow, but children's ministry has been much more vital in recent years. The old pastor knows what theological buzz words to avoid and which ones are safe. He knows these things, not because they are printed somewhere, but because he's been responsible for preaching and applying God's word in that place and to those people.

A search committee rarely has the knowledge necessary to be able to explain the particular theology of the church to incoming candidates. Instead they just paint with great big broad brushes or camp on theological minutiae. It's not really the search committee's fault. It's not supposed to be the guardian of theological truth or the equipper of the saints; that's the pastor's job.

The Search Committee Lacks the Right Knowledge of the Candidate

The search committee can learn things like where a minister went to school, how big his last church was, and what he thinks about certain ministry issues just by reading through his application. Those are all important things to know and will help weed out the wrong people, but there are certain things that a search committee can't know about a potential candidate.

In his article titled, *What's Wrong with Search Committees?* Mark Dever explains that search committees often have a fixation on credentials. "Degrees provide a commonly accepted currency of pastoral proficiency. But again, what may commonly be the case isn't always the case. Such artificial criteria for sorting through the volume of résumés can hide choice servants of God."[34]

They can't really discern his character based on an application and a few brief meetings. They can't know his theological hobbyhorses. They can't tell if he can connect with old people and young people. They can't know what kind of administrator he will be. They don't know his insecurities yet and can't see how they will affect his leadership style. There are just so many things that are impossible to know when a church has nothing but a search committee as its transition plan.

"We never would have hired him if we knew he was like that." That sentence has been uttered by far too many search committee members. Again, it's not really the committee's fault. It's just not reasonable to think that they would be able to know all of these things about the candidate. There are some things that only come to light through time and experience.

Search Committees Lack the Ability to Train

---

[34] Mark Dever, "What's Wrong With Search Committees?" *9Marks.com* http://9marks.org/article/whats-wrong-search-committees-part-1-2-finding-pastor/ (Accessed February 4, 2016)

Think back to a time in your life when you started a new job. The first day of that job was no doubt spent learning how things work. Even if it was a job doing something that you already knew how to do, you still needed to be trained on how to do it at the new place. Every job requires at least some measure of training. There's usually a supervisor or co-worker who will teach you the systems and procedures at that place of employment. There is someone you can go to for advice, to teach you how to run the coffee machine, or to tell you where the spare staples are located. The idea of hiring someone without offering any level of training is absurd.

In a *Forbes Magazine* article on succession in the business world Stephen Miles explains the need to "on-board the successor." He says, "There is no such thing as a 'ready now' candidate… Crucial support must be provided–a good team, wise and accessible mentors, executive coaching and a feedback-rich environment–to create a setting in which the new CEO can be the most effective. Directors have to remember that the search for a "ready now" candidate is a fool's errand."[35] The same rule goes for pastors. There is no such thing as a "ready now" pastoral candidate.

Churches hire new pastors every single day and have virtually nothing set up to train them. The man who was best equipped to do the training has already left. There's this mistaken idea that, just because a pastor has worked for ten years at another church, he

---

[35] Stephen Miles, "Succession Planning: How To Do It Right", *Forbes.com*, <http://www.forbes.com/2009/07/31/succession-planning-right-leadership-governance-ceos.html> (Accessed July 10, 2015).

doesn't need any training. It's a grave misconception on the part of the church.

An experienced pastor might not need remedial teaching about how to write a sermon or how to do a hospital visit, but they need a ton of advice on what to preach on and who they are visiting. Every new pastor needs to know the power structure of the church and how things get accomplished, because it's always different than what the organizational chart says. They need to be brought up to speed on the different members of the church and where the greatest challenges are going to come from. They need to know some backstories and some history.

The search committee is simply not designed to train the new pastor. It might be able to offer a demographic sketch of the church and a few pieces of advice, but most of the time the search committee doesn't even know what the new pastor needs to know. Their job was just to find him and hire him; he's on his own after that. This adds to the likelihood of the new pastor stepping on a landmine and blowing a leg off in the first six months of his ministry.

Those are just a few of the shortcomings of the search committee. The central problem is that a search committee simply can't fill the leadership void. The search committee isn't a suitable replacement for pastoral leadership in the church. When a pastor retires or resigns and hands the keys over to the board or the search committee he might think that he is transferring leadership at that point. But in reality what he is doing is creating a massive leadership void.

The board has never led the church. Why would pastors think that a board can lead through the most difficult transition the church has faced? The search committee is designed to manage things. Not even a weak leader would leave the important things in the hands of a committee. Pastors are called by God to lead and protect the church. They must not create a void in leadership by dumping the work of succession on the board or any other committee.

Thousands of churches are suffering, shrinking, and dying right now because good, godly pastors simply stopped leading. They abandoned their post and walked away. They listened to conventional wisdom that told them that it wasn't their job to lead through the process of succession. The problem is there is no one else in the world who is as equipped to do that tough job than the pastor.

God has appointed the pastor as the chief under shepherd, the steward, the caretaker, the earthly leader of that church. Do not dishonor that calling and do harm to the church body by neglecting to lead all the way to the very end. Right now, today, make a commitment to the long-term health of the church by vowing to lead through the process of developing a transition strategy. The second half of this book is dedicated to helping pastors understand what leadership through succession should look like.

Part 2

Making Transitions Healthier

Chapter 4

BIBLICAL LEADERSHIP LESSONS

A misdiagnosis can be deadly. Failure to properly identify the real problem will inevitably lead to a failure to treat it in the right way. Giving an aspirin to someone with a brain tumor might mask some symptoms, but it won't cure anything. How can we move beyond treating symptoms and find a cure for the heartache that so many churches feel during the point of transition?

The cure to what is ailing the church is not a better search committee or more assessments; the cure is simply better pastoral leadership. God has appointed the pastor as the guardian of the health of the church. The denomination can help, but it isn't their job. Committees might be useful, but a committee can't really lead anything. Assessments may help the pastor gain better insight into weak spots, but assessments are not the cure.

We need to move beyond treating symptoms and find the right cure. When it comes to better understanding what leadership should look like and especially the kind of leadership that leads to a healthy pastoral transition, the Bible has important lessons to teach us.

The Bible is full of great examples of godly leadership. Abraham led his family well. Solomon was a great king. The prophets pointed the people back to God. God has a track record of using faithful people to accomplish His will. The three biblical examples that we will look at all teach us some specific lessons about leadership in the midst of transition.

Moses & Joshua

It would be great if God would simply part the clouds and tell us who our successor is supposed to be. Plenty of prayer goes into the process. We know that God has a plan for His church, but the choice can be cloudy. If only God made it as easy for us as He did for Moses.

In Numbers 28:12-17, God instructed Moses to go up on a hill and look out over the Promised Land. God had already told Moses that he wouldn't be entering the Land, but God allowed him to at least see it. After looking out over the land Moses was "gathered to his people."

Moses didn't complain; he didn't argue with God; and he didn't try to negotiate. His first concern was for the people of God. He asked,

> May the LORD, the God of the spirits of all flesh, appoint a man over the congregation, who will go out and come in before them, and who will lead them out and bring them in,

68

so that the congregation of the LORD will not be like sheep which have no shepherd. (Num. 27:16-17, NASB)

After 40 years Moses knew better than anyone how stubborn and sinful the people were. They had been on the doorstep of the Promised Land before. He wanted to make sure that they wouldn't scatter after his death like sheep without a shepherd. Moses asked God for a successor.

It's possible that Moses knew who God had in mind. In Deuteronomy 1:38 and 3:28 God told Moses that Joshua would eventually lead the people. But Moses was wise enough at this point in his life to not make assumptions. He didn't want to run ahead of God or do things under his own authority; that kind of mistake is what got him barred from entering the Promised Land in the first place. So Moses asked God to be the one to name the next leader.

So the LORD said to Moses, "Take Joshua the son of Nun, a man in whom is the Spirit, and lay your hand on him; [19] and have him stand before Eleazar the priest and before all the congregation, and commission him in their sight. [20] You shall put some of your authority on him, in order that all the congregation of the sons of Israel may obey him. [21] Moreover, he shall stand before Eleazar the priest, who shall inquire for him by the judgment of the Urim before the

69

LORD. At his command they shall go out and at his command they shall come in, both he and the sons of Israel with him, even all the congregation."(Num. 27:18-21)

Joshua was the obvious choice. In Exodus 17, he had proved himself as a mighty warrior against Amalek. He had been the attendant to Moses since he was young (Num. 11:28). While the elders stayed at a distance, Joshua accompanied Moses up the mountain to receive the Ten Commandments (Exod. 24:13). When the pillar of cloud rested on the tent of meeting, and Moses spoke with God face to face, Joshua sat in that tent as the servant of Moses! (Exod. 33:9-11)

Moses spent years intentionally pouring his life into Joshua's with the knowledge that one day he would be gone and Joshua would need to step up and lead. Succession planning wasn't an afterthought for Moses. Moses spent those 40 years fighting for the people, interceding on their behalf, and protecting them from themselves. Even though the people of God did a lot of complaining and whining, Moses never gave up on them. It makes sense that their continued protection would be the first thing he thought about as he prepared to die.

The relationship between Moses and Joshua shows up in a number of places throughout Exodus, Numbers, and Deuteronomy.

These interactions between the leader and his successor teach us important lessons about how transitions should work.

Moses Brought Joshua Closer to God

It is absolutely amazing to me that, at a young age, Joshua was allowed into such close proximity to the presence of God. Moses must have known that to get too close to God would bring death. Yet Joshua was right there with Moses as he climbed Mt. Sinai and next to him as he sat engulfed in the presence of God in the Tent of Meeting. (Exod. 24:13; 33:11)

Moses didn't just teach Joshua about the law of God; he taught him about the reality of God. It is no wonder Joshua had no problem trusting that God would help the Israelites conquer the land, he had already seen God in a unique way and knew that God was powerful. Joshua's faith was deeper because Moses allowed him to see God at work firsthand.

In the same way pastors have the ability to do more than just teach people about theology or doctrine. They can offer more insight than how the baptismal works and where the extra communion cups are stored. Pastors have a unique ability to see all that God is doing in the midst of His church and His people. We see prayers answered and miracles occur. We see ministries start and grow in spite of our limitations. We see how God guides and directs in ways that ensure that He gets all the glory.

Most pastors do their best to communicate to the church all the ways that God is working, but there is a unique blessing that comes to someone who gets to see it from the inside. There's something gained through this process that can't be learned in school. The best pastors will help bring the next generation of leaders closer to God.

Moses Let Joshua Lead

In Exodus 17:8-13 Moses sends Joshua out to battle Amalek. It wasn't just a military battle; Moses knew that it was a spiritual battle as well. Moses trusted Joshua enough to let him lead. As Joshua and his army were fighting, where was Moses? He was stationed up on a hill, with his staff in his hand, arms raised up to God interceding on their behalf.

Joshua must have been fairly young when Moses chose him to be one of the 12 that would spy out the Promised Land. Moses placed the well-being of the whole nation into Joshua's hands. He and Caleb were the only ones who had the courage to stand up against the majority report and rally the people to go in and take the land.

In both of these examples, Moses sends Joshua into a dangerous situation and then does his best to support him and protect him. Moses understood that he hadn't been called to do everything; there were some leadership roles that others were better equipped for. Moses placed Joshua in these key leadership positions because he trusted Joshua and because he knew that Joshua would lead in more ways in the future.

Leadership ability is like a muscle that grows as it's used. Allowing other people to take the lead in the church not only helps them grow, it helps the pastor stay sane. The reality is that there are just some areas of ministry that we aren't going to be gifted for. We need to learn to trust others to step up and lead. This is a part of equipping the saints to do the work of ministry. It's not enough to just equip; we also need to get out of the way sometimes and let other people do the work. We need to encourage people to lead, and then do everything we can to support them and lift them up in prayer and help them to succeed.

Moses Encouraged Joshua

In Deuteronomy 1:38 and 3:28 God instructed Moses to "encourage" Joshua because he will one day be the leader of the people. The word "encourage" is the Hebrew word "Chazaq" which means to strengthen. Moses was called to equip, encourage, and build up Joshua for the purpose of making him into a great leader.

There's an ongoing debate about whether leaders are called or created. It seems that, at least in the case of Joshua, it was both. Joshua was chosen by God to be the next leader of the people of God. It was a choice that God had ordained a long time ago. But God understood that Joshua had some things he needed to learn before he would be ready for the job.

I'm not sure when God let Moses know that Joshua was going to be the next leader, but it was early enough that Moses had time to build Joshua up. God could have called another leader from inside a burning bush, but at that point in the life of the nation they needed continuity. God wanted there to be a smooth transition and for the nation to continue on in its mission.

Who are you building up? There is a really good chance that God has placed some young men in your church that have been marked for leadership. What are you doing to identify and build up these men? How are you working to make sure that leaders are molded and shaped to be ready when God calls them? How many opportunities have you missed out on to develop leaders simply because you weren't paying attention? Pray for God's wisdom and guidance as you encourage and build up the leaders around you.

Moses Taught Joshua

There are some particular lessons that Moses passed on to Joshua during their ministry together. One of these lessons is recorded in Numbers 11:25-29. The Spirit of God fell on the 70 elders and they prophesied for a period of time as a way of showing that God's Spirit was on them. In addition to the 70 elders, two other people got a dose of the Holy Spirit and also prophesied.

A report made its way back to Joshua and Moses that two men who are not official elders were prophesying in the camp. Joshua said to Moses, "Stop them!" Moses replied, "Are you jealous for my sake? Would that all the LORD'S people were prophets, that the LORD would put His Spirit upon them!" (Num. 11:29)

Moses took this opportunity to teach Joshua one of the most important lessons in leadership. Joshua saw the two men prophesying as a threat to Moses' leadership. In stark contrast to Aaron and Meriam who were jealous *of* Moses' leadership, Joshua was jealous *for* Moses.

Moses seemed appreciative that Joshua was willing to come to his defense, but Moses wasn't worried. He pointed Joshua back to the fact that God is the one who is in control and God is the one who deserves all the glory. It would be great if everyone had the Spirit of God on them! Wouldn't it be awesome if God caused the whole nation to prophesy? Moses taught Joshua that God is the one who is really in charge and that they merely serve Him.

Power struggles aren't something that the modern church invented. They've been happening for a long time. Moses had learned a few things through his experiences with various people who questioned his leadership and wanted to oust him. Moses learned that ultimately God is in control.

There is nothing more freeing and more important for a young leader to learn than the fact that he is not in control, and the board is not in control, and the grumblers are not in control. God is in control. He knows what He is doing. The more we learn to lean on His strength and not our own, the easier it will be to not freak out when things get tough.

Moses taught Joshua all about the law and about faith in God and about obedience; but he also taught Joshua that a leader is not independent, but a servant of God. There are many leadership lessons that God has taught you and wants you to pass on to the next generation. There are some lessons that can only be learned in the trenches as we faithfully serve God.

Moses Gives Joshua His Authority

Numbers 27:18-23 records Moses' last act as the leader of the people of God. He laid his hands on Joshua and transferred authority to him. In the presence of the priest and the entire congregation, Moses declared Joshua the God-appointed leader. He commissioned Joshua to continue to lead the people.

This act was the culmination of all the teaching, training, and equipping that Moses had been doing for years. It might have been obvious to everyone that Joshua was the next leader, but it wasn't something that was taken for granted. It is still important to make it perfectly clear that Moses was giving his blessing.

This selfless act of transferring leadership authority is something that doesn't happen often enough in the church. Transitions are more about handing off the keys and less about handing off authority. Every pastor, unless he has done a really bad job of leading that church, has a good measure of respect and authority available to pass on to the next man. He has an opportunity to love and protect the church one last time by making sure that the next pastor gets a head start.

When a pastor is disconnected from the process of training and selecting his successor, he has no real ability to offer this kind of blessing. Often, the outgoing leader would never have hired the person who is replacing him. He doesn't approve, let alone have any desire to transfer his authority. The outgoing pastor can't offer any kind of word of encouragement to the congregation because he has no idea who the new pastor is and what kind of leader he might be.

I took over for a pastor who had served the church for almost as many years as Moses led the Israelites. I spent considerable time learning from him and he gave me opportunities to lead. I understood his heart for the word of God and the people of God, and I shared his passion. When it was his time to step down, he was able to give me his blessing in front of the entire congregation. He had the ability to transfer some of his authority to me because of the investment that he had made in my life.

His blessing gave me a huge advantage. It was one of the things that enabled me to succeed in following a long-tenured pastor. His commissioning was honest and genuine and continued on past that transition point. He gave me something that no one else could have given me. He imparted more honor to me than a stack of degrees could have given. This honor would have been impossible for him to give had he not taken the time to invest in me.

Moses teaches us that strong leadership is essential, especially with an unhealthy congregation. When it was his time to die he made sure that the people would continue to have a strong, loving leader to guide them. Moses taught Joshua, invested in his life, and then, when the time was right, Moses passed his authority on to Joshua. Pastors today must follow Moses' example of a loving, wise leader.

Elijah & Elisha

Ministry is hard. I remember attending one of my first pastor retreats and listening in horror as the older pastors at the table compared scars from where their sheep had bitten them. Those pastors seemed so tired and discouraged and hurting. In the company of other pastors is one of the only places that they could talk about their pain.

As a young pastor who was still in the honeymoon phase and having a ton of fun serving my church, I felt a little guilty that I didn't have any stories of my own to share. The seasoned pastors assured me that I'd eventually understand what they were talking about. That prophetic word scared me, but I didn't fully believe them.

After nine years in the ministry I am still young and having a ton of fun serving in my church and I don't have any real horror stories, but I do understand better what they meant. Pastoral ministry is a unique and challenging calling. Pastor Art Azurdia says, "Pastoral ministry is exceedingly effective at making a man more acutely aware of his manifold inadequacies."[36]

It doesn't take a pastor long to realize that there's no way he has the ability to perfectly preach and teach and love the people in his church. That insecurity will either drive a man to strive for perfection, drive a man crazy, or drive a man to his knees. I realize that to accomplish the task that God has called me to I need to rely on His strength and power every single day.

Pastoral ministry is tiring. You are on call 24/7. You have a never ending list of people to visit. And you always have another sermon coming soon. There's a good amount of pressure that mounts week after week. Frustrating board meetings, where you have to think like a manager and wade through business, only add to the fatigue. Necessary administrative duties start to grow tiring over the years. Add to all of that people who are sinful and messy, and the ministry can leave even the strongest man worn out.

---

[36] Art Azurdia, *Spirit Empowered Preaching: The Vitality of the Holy Spirit in Preaching* (Fearn, Ross-shire, Great Britain: Mentor, 1998), 19.

Perhaps one of the harshest stories of ministry burnout in the Bible is found in 1 Kings 19. The prophet Elijah found himself running for his life, hiding under a bush and too depressed to even eat. He uttered the same words that many pastors have no doubt uttered at some point, "I have had enough, Lord". He was so discouraged that he just wanted God to take his life. Things weren't working, he was no good at the job, and he felt tired and scared and done. He fell asleep in an attempt to escape. Most pastors can empathize with Elijah!

What makes Elijah's depression so stark is the fact that just a few verses earlier he experienced a miraculous victory. In chapter 18 he made a mockery of the prophets of Baal and showed that only God is real and alive and powerful. God sent fire from heaven that consumed the altar and the people all bowed down and declared, "The Lord - He is God! The Lord - He is God!" Elijah had the prophets of Baal arrested and slaughtered.

Elijah had been used by God in a mighty way! But when Jezebel found out she vowed to kill him. At this point Elijah must have felt like everything he had done had been in vain. It didn't really matter that he had embarrassed the prophets of Baal and had them killed. In the end, what had he accomplished? Elijah cried out to God: "I have been very zealous for the LORD, the God of hosts; for the sons of Israel have forsaken Your covenant, torn down Your altars and killed Your prophets with the sword. And I alone am left; and they seek my life, to take it away." (1 Kgs. 19:10)

Elijah swung from the height of victory and success to the depth of discouragement and depression. I did everything You asked me to do God! I did my part, but those people have forsaken You, dishonored You, killed Your prophets, and now they want to kill me! Elijah was ready to give up.

However, God was not done with Elijah yet. His ministry wasn't over. It wasn't his time to die or retire. It's important to note that God didn't get mad at Elijah for running and hiding. Elijah was not scolded for his discouragement. Instead God went to some supernatural lengths to strengthen and build him up. First, God provided for Elijah's physical needs. He sent an angel to get him to eat and drink. God kept his body going.

Next, God drew near to Elijah. He talked with him, comforted him, and even offered to show Elijah His presence. Then God gave Elijah a mission: go anoint Hazael as king over Aram; go anoint Jehu as king of Israel; and go anoint Elisha as your successor. Finally, God let Elijah know that the enemies of God will be defeated, a faithful remnant still exists, and God has a future for them.

It's interesting to note, of the three things that God told Elijah to do, he only completed one of them - the appointment of Elisha. It was Elisha who ultimately anointed Hazael and Jehu. The very first thing that Elijah did as he headed down from his mountain of despair was to find Elisha and toss his mantle on him.

So he departed from there and found Elisha the son of Shaphat, while he was plowing with twelve pairs of oxen before him, and he with the twelfth. And Elijah passed over to him and threw his mantle on him. [20] He left the oxen and ran after Elijah and said, "Please let me kiss my father and my mother, then I will follow you." And he said to him, "Go back again, for what have I done to you?" [21] So he returned from following him, and took the pair of oxen and sacrificed them and boiled their flesh with the implements of the oxen, and gave it to the people and they ate. Then he arose and followed Elijah and ministered to him.(1 Kgs. 19:19-21)

The middle of a ministry breakdown seems like a really weird place to talk about succession planning. Why did God choose that time to instruct Elijah to go find his replacement? Wouldn't some good food and divine encouragement have been enough to get Elijah back on track? Wouldn't it have made more sense to worry about succession at a later point? Elijah still had seven fruitful years of ministry left ahead of him!

I believe the reason that God sent Elijah to anoint Elisha is found in the last sentence in verse 21: "Then he[Elisha] arose and followed Elijah and ministered to him." I believe that God sent Elijah to choose his successor because God knew that Elijah needed to be ministered to! He had faithfully served for years and still had some work left to do, but he wouldn't have to walk that road alone.

There's no doubt that Elisha would benefit greatly from having Elijah as his mentor, but Elijah also received a huge blessing from the relationship. Ministers need to be ministered to. This truth is especially true towards the end of a long ministry run. The mentor-student relationship benefits both the old pastor and the new pastor. But the way we do ministry in this country today often precludes us from ever experiencing this kind of blessing. Instead, tired pastors just burn out or phone it in or run away.

There are a few fundamental lessons on succession planning that we can glean from the way God guided Elijah and Elisha.

God Ordains a Man

As with Moses and Joshua, God ultimately appointed Elijah's successor. Both Moses and Elijah simply paid attention to God's guidance. They had a huge role to play in teaching and training and equipping the next leader, but it was God's choice.

In my two case studies, both churches had people on their search committees that prayed. But one group didn't just pray for guidance, they actively sought it out. They were open to things turning out different than they might have planned. They didn't allow preconceived preferences or printed guidelines to limit them. They expected God to open and close doors and lead them to the right choice.

The other group did plenty of praying, but stuck to the guidelines they were given. They began with an idea of the kind of pastor they wanted and deserved and never deviated from that idea. In their prayers they told God what they wanted, but failed to leave room for God to tell them what He wanted.[37]

God isn't going to part the clouds and tell you who to throw your mantle on, like He did for Elijah, but that doesn't mean that God is silent. God can and does guide when we get out of the way and make room for Him to take the lead. That requires more than just the ability to pray, but also the ability to listen.

A Man is Often Called First and Trained Second

God knew that Joshua would one day lead the people, long before Moses' death. Elisha was called right off the farm. Many of Jesus' disciples were called to drop their fishing nets and follow Him. Timothy was called at a young age to serve with Paul. It makes sense that a calling into the ministry precedes training for ministry.

That's still supposed to be the way things are done; however, in our modern educational system people often pursue theological

---

[37] Both churches started with age and experience requirements, but one of the churches was willing to alter their requirements when God brought a younger man to the church. The full case study is in the appendix.

84

training first and then try to figure out where they are called, or *if* they are called. Training for full-time ministry that is devoid of a calling from God to full-time ministry service is a waste of time and money.

Unfortunately, colleges and seminaries are not equipped to discern whether or not someone is called. In theory, seminaries should be full of people who have been called by God and commissioned by a church or missions organization. They should be places that help the church do the work of doctrinal and theological training within the context of ministry. But somehow seminaries became disconnected from the church, and biblical education became a separate commodity that wasn't necessarily united with a calling.

However, churches usually look to seminaries to produce men who are properly trained and called. In reality the seminary doesn't do the calling, and only does a portion of the training. The confirmation of a ministry call and much of the ministry training has to occur in the church. More seminaries, like Western Seminary (shameless plug), are realizing that their purpose is to serve the church. They have created internships and mentorships that help to develop a closer link with the church. They offer distance learning opportunities and in-ministry tracks that are designed to educate those people who have been called and are actively serving in the church.

I understand that "The Calling" can be tough to pin down. It's not a black and white kind of thing, but it is still a real thing. It's a biblical thing. It's not arbitrary. It is something that can be discovered and confirmed. And, very often, the kinds of people that God calls are different than the kinds of people we have in mind. If a church thinks that the only men who are called by God are those who have spent three to five years in a seminary and are already "trained," then they will miss out on some great leaders!

The Successor Will be Different

The differences in personality between Elijah and Elisha are so significant that just about every commentary mentions them. These differences were primarily superficial, but still notable.

Elijah was shaggy and unkempt; Elisha was clean cut. Elijah wore a sheepskin mantle; Elisha wore normal clothes of the day. Elijah lived much of his life isolated from people; Elisha had a house in town. Elijah had some periods of depression and discouragement, while Elisha just kept serving faithfully. Elijah was probably an introvert; Elisha was probably more of an extrovert. Even with the differences, both men were effective servants of God.

There were a lot of things that were very different about the two, but the thing that wasn't different was their calling from God and their empowerment as prophets. They both preformed miracles and had a profound influence on the nation. They both were faithful men who served well.

The superficial differences didn't matter that much because of their similarities in the important things. Unfortunately, too often, when a new pastor begins, the personality differences are jarring to the congregation. He doesn't last long enough to demonstrate that he is just as faithful and loving as the former pastor. It was in the context of working alongside of Elijah that Elisha showed himself to be trustworthy and faithful.

As pastors we must be willing to work with people who are very different than we are. That is not easy! However, if leaders take the time to understand and love someone in spite of their differences, they will teach the rest of the congregation how to do the same thing.

This probably seems obvious, but often the main reason that pastors fail to invest in training and mentoring their successor is because of personality differences. They can't seem to get past the superficial level and get to a place of mutual respect and passion for the mission. It takes humility and a clear focus on the things that really matter to God to be able to work with someone who is different than you. But here's the thing - everyone is different than you.

Training Your Successor is a Blessing for Both of You

If pastors continue to believe that they should not have any involvement in the succession process, they will continue to deprive themselves and their successors of huge blessings. God has given us an amazing gift that we have abandoned in favor of a secular business model, which doesn't even work anymore. There are very real benefits that come from personally training a successor.

Elijah was tired, burned out, and depressed, but not finished yet. Elisha was more than just a replacement for Elijah; he was refreshment. Elisha ministered to Elijah, and Elijah ministered to Elisha. They both received something from the relationship. Elisha learned God's word and grew in faith and wisdom, and Elijah gained renewed purpose and a companion in the work. Elisha served as a living and breathing reminder that there was still hope and a future for the people of God. Elisha made Elijah a better leader, and Elijah helped set Elisha on a course to be an even greater leader.

I interviewed my predecessor who served our church for 37 years before me. I asked him if there was ever a time when he felt like quitting. He said, "Oh yes, all the time. A couple of times I was very serious about leaving." He went on to explain that the first time he thought about leaving was just a few years into his ministry. Things weren't growing much and he started to wonder if maybe he wasn't the right man for the job. Right at that time, three key men were saved and started actively serving in the church. Those ministry partnerships gave him the encouragement he needed to keep going.

The second time was 25 years into the ministry. There was an ugly shakeup in the church that involved the sin of a staff member followed by controversy in with music (I'm sure none of you can relate). The end result was the loss of staff and the loss of some close friends. At that point he actually looked around at other churches. This time it was the assistance of the youth pastor (of all people!) who stepped up and filled in the gap with worship that encouraged him.

Pastors grossly underestimate how much they need other people. We may even pride ourselves on being the solitary rock who has to carry the weight of the world. We wear our weariness like a badge of honor. We don't take advantage of the blessings that come from serving together, shoulder to shoulder, with someone younger, eager to learn, and excited to minister.

The relationship between Elijah and Elisha teaches us that succession planning isn't just about leaving the church in capable hands; it's one way that God encourages and blesses a pastor after years of faithful service. Ministry is weighty and wearying. There is renewed joy and excitement when we allow someone to help share the load.

Paul and Timothy

Timothy was the son of a Greek father and Jewish mother. His mother and grandmother instilled in him from a young age a genuine faith in God. It's likely that Timothy first heard the gospel during Paul's first missionary journey. Timothy already had a background of faith, but upon hearing the gospel of Jesus Christ he not only became a Christian, but also a faithful servant.

Timothy joined in the missionary work of Paul. He learned from Paul's example and grew in his knowledge of Jesus' teaching. It wasn't long before Timothy was sent out to different churches as an encourager. Timothy was sent to the church in Corinth to remind them of Paul's faithful example. Paul also sent Timothy to the church at Philippi to cheer them on in person. Paul understood that Timothy genuinely loved the people in that community and was concerned for their welfare. Too many people seek after their own personal interests, not those of Jesus, but Timothy was different. He served with Paul as a son serving with a father.

Almost every time Paul wrote of Timothy he referred to him as a beloved son (1 Cor. 4:17, Phil. 2:22, 1 Tim. 1:2, 2 Tim. 1:2). Their relationship was much deeper than just a teacher with a student. They were friends and co-laborers who served with humility. Clearly Paul understood there was a mutual blessing that comes with the mentor relationship.

Timothy was far from perfect. He was young, fearful, timid, and nervous. He wasn't exactly the kind of man you would expect to carry on the mantle of leadership from Paul, a man who was bold and courageous. Despite Timothy's weaknesses, he was humble and faithful. Those were the qualities that Paul observed that led him to appoint Timothy as the pastor to the church in Ephesus.

Paul spent years mentoring Timothy. Paul showed him what faithful ministry looked like. Then Paul gave Timothy opportunities to minister to people. Finally, Paul appointed Timothy to be the shepherd in one of Paul's most beloved churches. Even after sending Timothy off on his own, Paul still sent letters to teach and encourage him.

The two Pastoral Epistles written to Timothy are filled with helpful guidelines for church management. But the relationship behind these letters is every bit as important to understand. They serve as a model for us today. There is a tremendous blessing that comes from the mentorship relationship. It goes beyond the mere development of skills. It involves imparting our love for Jesus and the church to the next generation.

John Macarthur says, "Every true leader can thank God when by His grace He gives us spiritual children who are like Timothy, reproductions of ourselves. In the best cases, they become even better than we are, more devoted than we are, more godly than we are."[38]

Pastors have missed out on this huge blessing! Don't leave leadership training or mentoring up to seminaries or professors. God has called you to be a leader and to train leaders! We can learn from Paul's relationship with Timothy.

It Doesn't Have to be Complicated

My guess is that Paul never thought of what we was doing with Timothy as "succession planning." He was simply making disciples, passing on his knowledge, and training up faithful men who could continue the work after he was gone. Paul was smart enough to know that, for the gospel to spread, it would take people like Timothy continuing to teach and preach.

Paul's strategy wasn't complicated: "The things which you have heard from me in the presence of many witnesses, entrust these to faithful men who will be able to teach others also."(2 Tim. 2:2) There's a chain that leads from Paul to Timothy to other faithful men and then to others after them. Paul instructed Timothy to train leaders who would also train leaders. That process should endure until Jesus comes back.

Sometimes we can make the whole process more complicated than it needs to be. If we are pastors who are teaching and training other men who we know will be able to train the people who come

---

[38] John MacArthur, *The Book on Leadership* (Nashville, TN: Nelson Books, 2004), 189

after them, then our churches will be just fine. It's when we leave leadership development up to someone else or fail to do our job of entrusting the truth to other faithful men that the system breaks down.

I love that Paul doesn't get too prescriptive or overly complicated with his instruction to Timothy. Just keep passing that leadership baton to the next man.

Don't be Afraid of Young Eagles

Paul tells Timothy, "Let no one look down on your youthfulness, but *rather* in speech, conduct, love, faith *and* purity, show yourself an example of those who believe."(1 Tim. 4:12) There has always been a tendency to look down on those who are young. Timothy probably wasn't very old when he was appointed as the pastor in Ephesus, but there's no doubt he was qualified. He had been brought up in the faith, had given his life to Christ, was tutored by Paul, had proven to have a deep love for people, and was knowledgeable about the truth.

Churches today often look down on young men who desire to preach and lead as a senior pastor. There's a lack of confidence in younger men because they do not have as much proven experience. Often men are expected to put in time as a youth pastor or associate pastor before they can get a shot at a senior pastor role.

Pastor Larry Osborne has written extensively about the importance of letting young eagles fly. He points out our tendency as old and seasoned leaders to look down on the next generation as immature and ineffective. We forget that we used to be young and impatient and eager at one time too. Instead of being frustrated or afraid of their youth, they need to be given the freedom to fly.

Osborne warns,

> I'd be a liar if I said that protecting and promoting young eagles is a pain-free venture. It's far easier in theory than in practice. I don't like giving up my personal power, prestige, or preferences any more than the next guy does.
>
> But young eagles are born to fly. It's their nature. It's how God made them. If they can't fly high in our church, they'll bolt and fly elsewhere. And sadly, if and when they do, they'll take most of the life, vitality, and the future of the church with them.[39]

Timothy proved that he had the character and the heart to be a pastor. Paul knew that he would preach the truth faithfully. Even though Timothy was young, he was eager to serve God. Paul was never threatened by Timothy's youth; instead, Paul encouraged Timothy and gave him the freedom to fly.

---

[39] Osborne, 115.

Succession is More about Building a Relationship than Finding a Replacement

This may be the greatest tragedy in our modern day methods of pastoral transitions: it is viewed as nothing more than filling a staff position. It's an HR problem. It's a job search. But it should be so much more than that!

Paul and Timothy had a close relationship; like a father with his son, like two friends on mission together. It was in the context of that close mentoring and serving relationship that Timothy learned how to be a great pastor and Paul gained the confidence to put him in charge of one of his favorite churches.

Just like the close relationship between Moses and Joshua, and Elijah and Elisha, Paul and Timothy had a close relationship. That relationship was a blessing to both of them. The relationship made the process of leadership transition natural and fluid. Their relationship wasn't primarily for the purpose of replacement planning, but just joyfully serving God together.

Many churches face problems when the time comes for their pastor to leave, stemming from the fact that no ministry relationships have been formed. The process of handing off authority isn't natural and fluid, but clunky and painful. There is no relationship that enables the outgoing pastor to commend his replacement.

How are you, as a pastor, seeking to build relationships with the next generation of leaders? Has God led someone across your path who, like Timothy, is eager, faithful, and willing to learn? How can you be more intentional about building that kind of relationship? What would it look like to not worry about who will replace you and just work on building relationships?

Your Work Doesn't End When Your Successor is in Place

Paul's mentoring relationship with Timothy didn't end when Timothy took on the role of pastor. 1 and 2 Timothy were both written after Timothy was installed as the pastor. Paul continued to encourage and build up Timothy. He offered words of instruction and exhortation, acted as a cheerleader, and gave advice about how to shape and structure the church.

Paul wrote to remind Timothy of the dangers of false prophets. Even though Timothy had a firm grasp on the truth, as a leader in the church he faced surprising opposition and people who tried to deceive the flock. Timothy needed to be vigilant to keep preaching the truth in a hostile environment. Paul's words helped cement Timothy's doctrinal foundation.

Paul also reminded Timothy of his calling. Every pastor will face insecurity and doubt, especially when things get hard. Paul reminded Timothy that he had been called by God and had every reason to be courageous and strong. He has been given a spirit of courage, not timidity. Though Timothy might have felt young, inexperienced, and over his head at times, his mentor reminded him that God had given him everything he needed to succeed.

Paul wrote to teach Timothy how to establish other leaders around him who could help with the work of ministry. He also wrote to help Timothy deal with different personalities in the church. Faithful management of resources and people is an important part of the role of pastor. Paul made sure that Timothy had basic guidelines to use in his leadership role.

I don't know if these letters to Timothy were written in response to questions that Timothy had, or if Paul just knew what Timothy would need to hear. But I can imagine that Timothy kept these letters very close. He read them, followed their instruction, and gained strength from them. No one other than Paul could have offered such specific and detailed advice, because he knew Timothy and he knew the church in Ephesus.

Paul also helped Timothy by saying nice things about him. Paul wanted to make sure others knew that Timothy was supported, called, and gifted. Paul told the Corinthians, "Now if Timothy comes, see that he is with you without cause to be afraid, for he is doing the Lord's work, as I also am. So let no one despise him. But send him on his way in peace".(1 Cor. 16:10-11) In a number of places in Scripture, Paul made a point to acknowledge and commend Timothy. He intentionally urged others to respect him and support him as a co-laborer with Paul. Paul did everything in his power to see Timothy succeed in ministry.

In the same way, the pastor's job of guarding and blessing his church doesn't end when he stops being the pastor there. There will likely be a need for him to continue to instruct and encourage his successor after he is gone. There are things that only the pastor knows about that church. There are particular landmines that he can help the new pastor avoid. There are difficult personalities that he can warn the new pastor about.

The ability to continue to guide the next pastor is only possible if there is a relationship that exists first. The two case studies found in the appendix illustrate a marked difference in the level of involvement of the two outgoing pastors. In the church that failed, the outgoing pastor had no contact with the new pastor at all. No relationship was formed, no attempt was made to offer any words of warning or advice, and the new pastor had no desire to seek any advice. The end result was disastrous! In the second church the veteran pastor had a close mentoring relationship with the new pastor that started before he left and continued on for years after his retirement.

Timothy would have failed if he was merely viewed as Paul's replacement. Timothy was not as old or wise or gifted as Paul. The contrasts would have eventually led to his failure. But Timothy wasn't just a replacement, he was Paul's successor. He had the benefit of spring-boarding off of Paul's years of ministry investment. Timothy's ministry was elevated as he was lifted up by Paul.

Pastor, do you see your job as helping to elevate the next man to success? Are you willing to continue to encourage and support your replacement even after you have left the church? I know that this process will take extra time and energy, but there are things that your replacement will need desperately to survive that only you can give him.

Conclusion

There is no biblically mandated method for doing succession planning. Even the three examples we looked at were not identical. There is room for variation based on culture, customs, and pastoral strengths. Although there is no paint-by-numbers methodology, the Bible consistently presents transition planning as an important leadership trait.

Chapter 5

THREE STAGES OF SUCCESSION

This book isn't really intended to be a detailed procedural manual. It's more of a call to action. My hope is that I can convince pastors to take the lead in planning for their successor. The details of how to accomplish that goal are largely up to you. Every church is different, every denomination has different hurdles, and every pastor has different gifts. There is not one right way.

Vanderbloemen and Bird point out, "Succession is a process, not an event. It's a leadership value and practice…There are very few cardinal rules in succession. It's much more an art than a science."[40] Healthy transitions happen as a part of the natural outflow of good pastoral leadership. So the cardinal rule is that pastors need to take the lead in this area. The old rule that says pastors shouldn't be involved wrongly views succession as an event. Instead, leaders are needed to help guide the whole process.

Even though there isn't a cookie cutter method for success, there are some general guidelines that we can follow. There are some steps that pastors can take that will prevent their church from entering into a tailspin when they leave. There are three distinct phases of

---

[40] Vanderbloemen and Bird, 29.

succession planning that every pastor will eventually face. In each of these phases there are things that a pastor can do to help lead and guide his church. The specific things he does in each phase will depend on his unique church and his unique gifts as a pastor. The worst thing he could do in each stage is nothing.

Stage 1: Preparing for Departure

Pastors enter into this phase the very first day they begin their tenure. From that point on they are moving towards the day when God will call them to a different church, or retirement, or something else. Vanderbloemen and Bird rightly state, "Every pastor is an interim".[41] We are all temporary. Hopefully we will be able to serve for many years, but eventually our turn will be over and someone else will take our place.

Succession planning is all about leadership development. It is about finding and training the right person to take over for you. It is way more complex than a mere replacement plan. The process takes more time and intentionality.

Even if you don't plan on leaving your church any time soon, you still have a responsibility to set the stage. Because none of us knows how long God will have us at our church or on this earth we

---

[41] Vanderbloemen and Bird, 9.

need to plan ahead. A good leader looks to the future and casts a vision.

Here are a few of the things that you need to do in in this phase of your ministry.

Pray and Evaluate

Spend a healthy amount of time talking to God about this issue. What do you sense as God's plan for your ministry? Will you be at your church for the rest of your career? Are you planning to move on in a few years? Are there some leadership skills that you need to acquire? What does God's word have to say about your responsibility to the church? Are there areas of pride or fear that God needs to remove from your heart?

As you pray, honestly evaluate your personal ability to train and equip the next leader. Evaluate your unique church context and determine what resources you have to work with. Think about potential leaders within your church right now who might have ministry potential. Pray about what the next steps might look like.

One criticism that some of the denominational leaders shared is that most pastors aren't very strategic. They don't do a good job of thinking ahead and preparing in an intentional way for the future. Part of the reason is that the job is so demanding that it is hard enough to keep up with the day to day responsibilities. Finding time to slow down and think about the future of the church is simply a luxury that most pastors don't have.

I know how hard it can be to find the time to think past the next sermon. But as a leader you need to carve out time to pray and plan. What would happen to the church if you got hit by a truck? Are there people that God has put across your path who seem to have a huge amount of ministry potential? Are you being a responsible steward of the church that you have been entrusted with?

Talk About It!

First, talk to your spouse or a trusted friend about what it will look like when you leave. Talking things out with family and friends is a safe first step. There's no doubt that this is a scary subject, so starting the conversation in a safe place is good. It's likely that your spouse has her own set of questions and worries involving the future. Talking those things through together is healthy.

Don't limit the conversation to your family, take the next step and share it with your board or leadership team. Maybe the safest next step is to talk about it with your staff. It might come as a surprise to many of you, but members of the congregation, your staff, and your board have already been wondering about your departure. It doesn't matter if you are young or old, the people in your church are curious about your intentions.

If you are a young pastor your church wants to know if you plan on sticking around or leaving. Consistency and commitment are highly valued and the church wants to know that you are committed to them. No church wants to be used as a step ladder to the next thing or feel like they are being used. They want to know that you love the church and the community as much as they do.

If you are an older pastor your church is starting to get worried about what the future will hold. The other staff members are wondering if they will get a chance to take the lead, or they are concerned about what the next leader will be like. People want to know what's going to happen next, and they are looking to you to provide the answers.

Pastor, you need to be the one to start this conversation. Put it on the agenda for your next board meeting. Reach out to a denominational leader to help you think through the process. Be clear and open and honest with your staff and board about your personal plans. Be clear with them that the reason for the discussion is not because you are anxious to leave, but because you are committed to the health of the church.

Even though I'm strongly advocating that the pastor take the lead in succession planning, I absolutely don't recommend that he does it all alone. God has given you a board and other staff to help you lead well. Something this important requires a team effort. You are called to be the leader of that team. They have valuable insight and important questions to consider. Talking things out helps you and your whole church plan well.

Create an Emergency Plan

In *Next*, the authors describe the importance of planning for emergencies or unforeseen departures. "Form a plan, write it down, and have your board collaborate with and/or approve the plan. Now ask each staff or key volunteer to create their own 'hit by a bus' plan for their own succession."[42] Who would preach? Who would take the lead? Who would take care of all the administrative duties? Who would keep the mission moving forward? Will the time of shock and mourning be followed by stability and strength, or even more chaos and confusion?

As the senior pastor you might have your own ideas about who would take charge, but if those ideas have never been communicated or confirmed, they are worthless. Is everyone on the same page? Does the person you think should take the lead know that it is expected? Does the board know who to call in case of an emergency? Does the rest of the congregation understand who the second in command is?

In a large church there might be five or six different people who could step up in a crisis. If none of them know who is supposed to

---

[42] Vanderbloemen and Bird, 33-34.

fill the leadership void, there is a risk that they will all defer to each other or all jockey for the position. Without any plan in place the risk of a leadership struggle or a leadership void increases.

In smaller churches the problem is identifying someone who could handle the weight of the responsibility. Smaller churches don't have the luxury of multiple staff members who can jump into action. The emergency leader will likely be a board member or lay member of the church. Do they know what to do if something happens to you?

There is a huge benefit to those churches that are a part of a particular denomination or association of churches. Those partnerships are a great source of support and advice in the midst of a storm. They can help appoint an interim preacher, offer structural guidance, and even financial assistance. If you are a small church with no one who could handle the ministry responsibilities, then your emergency plan might be simply a phone number of the regional director for your denomination. For a non-denominational church there are a number of great agencies that can help with pulpit supply.

Whether you are the pastor of a large church or a small church, there will be some work that you need to do to ensure whoever takes your place will be ready. The emergency plan should go further than just a name in an envelope. Next, there must be some investment of time and energy to train and equip that person for the task.

Create a Leadership Pipeline

In *The Leadership Baton*, the authors discuss what it looks like for a church to have a culture of leadership development. It isn't just a succession strategy for the senior pastor, but something that every staff member and ministry leader is actively involved in. "Empower every leader to be on the lookout for his or her replacement. Train your leaders to develop prospective leaders through coaching, mentoring, and encouragement. Either figuratively or literally, give every leader a baton."[43]

When there is a culture of leadership development that permeates every area of the church then the discussion about training a pastoral replacement won't be awkward or uncomfortable, but obvious and natural. When you train others to search for and equip their replacements within the church it gives you greater ability to search for and train your replacement.

Vanderbloemen and Bird also talk about the importance of creating a culture of leadership development. "Intentionally build a leadership pipeline by making relationship-based leadership development a regular part of your planning, programming, and budgeting... A church-wide culture of leadership development will not only help your church in its current mission but will also help develop potential future successors."[44]

---

[43] Forman, Jones, and Miller, 37.
[44] Vanderbloemen and Bird, 35.

One of the most important things that you can do right now to ensure a healthy transition when the time comes is to create a leadership culture in your church. It not only helps to solve the never ending problem of not having enough volunteers, it is also a biblical expectation.

Before Paul wrote to encourage Timothy as he ministered in Ephesus, Paul wrote these words to that church:

And He gave some as apostles, and some as prophets, and some as evangelists, and some as pastors and teachers, [12] for the equipping of the saints for the work of service, to the building up of the body of Christ; [13] until we all attain to the unity of the faith, and of the knowledge of the Son of God, to a mature man, to the measure of the stature which belongs to the fullness of Christ. (Eph. 4:11-13)

God's word is very clear that the purpose of a leader is to help equip and train up others. This process of leadership reproduction is what helps the church continue to thrive from generation to generation. Paul is not merely talking about equipping people to teach Sunday school or serve on committees, he is telling leaders to help people reach their full potential in Christ.

Is there someone in your church right now that God is calling to pastoral ministry? Are there some things that you can do to confirm their call? What can you do to educate and equip them? What kind of training do they need? How can you give them opportunities to grow through preaching or teaching? Is there a Joshua or an Elisha that God has placed in your life?

Creating a leadership pipeline is tougher to do in the small church. You don't have as much depth on the bench. But in some ways it is even more crucial for the small church pastor to invest time in developing leaders. It's much harder to draw from the outside in a small church, especially in a rural community. If you are close enough to a college or seminary those might be resources for interns and people looking for ministry experience.

We need to stop viewing succession planning as searching for a replacement and start to think of it as building a relationship. As pastors we must look for young men to come alongside and encourage. Even if they end up serving at a different church or heading off to start their own church, the investment is still worth it!

A healthy leadership pipeline enables us to give young men an opportunity to develop their ministry skills. Not every 25-year-old that feels called to ministry feels called to youth ministry. There are some who have a passion at an early age to preach and teach the word of God to adults. Forcing younger men to put in their time in an associate position when God has called them to preach and lead is a bad idea.

In both of the case studies that I investigated God called a young, relatively inexperienced man to be the next pastor.[45] Part of the struggle at First Baptist Church (FBC) came from the arrogant idea that the church deserved someone older and more experienced. They mistakenly believed that the best thing for them was a veteran outsider. In the end it was a rookie insider with a love for the church and community that brought healing and stability.

Create a leadership pipeline in your church that strives to discover God's calling in the lives of the people that He has brought your way. Do your part to equip and encourage them, and then put them into action!

Create a Financial Plan

If you are a senior pastor, you have a huge responsibility to be a good steward of the resources that God has entrusted to you. Not just the church's resources, but your own as well. Planning for the future means having a financial plan that will enable the church to afford the costs of succession, and it means having a personal financial plan that will provide for your needs when you leave.

First, at an early age you need to have some kind of retirement plan in place. The church is notorious for not paying pastors well and not providing for the future. A pastor with kids, a mortgage, and

---

[45] The case study is detailed in the appendix

the usual expenses will have a tough time saving money. It's hard enough just to make ends meet from month to month. It takes discipline to make sure that you have a safety net in place that could support you during a pastoral transition or retirement.

In an article titled "What Happens When Boomer Pastors Retire?" Thom Rainer points out that there is a large bubble of baby boomer pastors who are nearing the age of retirement. He's finding that many of them don't think they need to retire until well after age 65 and many don't have the financial means to retire. This will likely cause added frustration in many churches.[46]

As the leader you need to help your church understand the value of establishing some kind of retirement fund for you. It is in the church's best interest to ensure that their pastor has the freedom to step down when the time is right.

Vanderbloemen and Bird warn, "Far too many pastors face retirement with no way to fund it. This reality can wreck a succession before it even begins."[47] A stark reality is that many pastors cling too tightly to their job simply because they need the money. "The Lesson for younger pastors is that personal finances cannot be overlooked as an important and ongoing foundation to a future succession decision. The challenge for pastors of all ages is to

---

[46] Thom S. Rainer, "What Happens When Boomer Pastors Retire?" *ThomRainer.com* <http://thomrainer.com/2014/09/happens-boomer-pastors-retire/> (Accessed December 5, 2015)
[47] Vanderbloemen and Bird, 45.

live on less than you earn so that you can give generously and save diligently."[48]

One of the greatest gifts that you can give your church is financial responsibility. You owe it to your family and to your congregation to make sure that you are secure.

Second, as the leader of the church you have a responsibility to help your church budget for succession. The process will require an investment. Too often the church fails to accurately count the costs. Failure to invest wisely from the beginning inevitably results in paying a much bigger price in the end.

In *The Elephant In The Board Room*, an entire chapter is devoted to helping churches count the costs. They explain how the loss of an effective pastor will result in a 15 percent drop in attendance and eventually in giving.[49] If the process of finding a new pastor takes a year or so that loss is compounded and a rebound in giving doesn't happen immediately after a new pastor is hired. Add to all that the normal costs incurred by the search committee and the likely increased salary for the new pastor and the total cost for finding a replacement is huge! A medium sized church could see a price tag in the hundreds of thousands associated with a transition! And that's if things go well!

---

[48] Vanderbloemen and Bird, 45-46.
[49] Weese and Crabtree, 30.

Botched transitions will incure far greater costs. The normal 15 percent drop in attendance and giving will grow to something closer to 50 percent, or worse. With the volunteer pool gone, ministries will dry up and any potential for growth will evaporate. Often existing staff members have to be let go or look for a different church. It is not uncommon for a vibrant stable church to come very close to death within a few short years of a leadership transition.

This was the case with FBC. They entered into the search process full of excitement and anticipation. The church was growing and strong. They never thought that in less than five years it would be on the brink of closure. Ultimately, failure to invest in and properly plan for succession nearly led them to financial ruin.

It will require a financial investment to hire someone with the goal of equipping them to take over for you, but the upfront cost will be less than what your church will lose during the time that they are searching for a new leader, even if the replacement pastor isn't a dud. If the new pastor doesn't work out, for any reason, the costs will skyrocket.

The benefit of hiring and training your replacement is that it results in a smooth and seamless transition. There is no 15 percent drop in attendance and giving caused by a leadership void because there is no lag between one leader and the next. There is a far greater likelihood of success for the new pastor because he has already been vetted and acclimated. He already loves the church and they love him.

Children's ministry, women's ministry, men's ministry, seniors' ministry, and youth ministry are all important parts of the church. Missions, outreach, and advertising are all things that a healthy church will invest money in. But none of these things has the potential to destroy a church as quickly as a poor leadership transition does. I know that it feels weird and it's "not the way we've always done it", but setting aside money to invest in your next pastor is simply being a good steward of what God has entrusted to you.

Decrease So That Others Can Increase

It was John the Baptist who verbalized this truth, "He must increase but I must decrease." (John 3:30) The concept is foundational to great leadership. This is a reality that we see exemplified often in Scripture. This kind of slow fade is at the heart of every level 5 leader. The ability to allow someone else to have the reigns requires humility.

John the Baptist had built a thriving ministry out in the wilderness. He had a lot of people listening to him and coming to be baptized. When Jesus began his ministry a lot of people left John to follow Jesus. John understood that his ministry role was simply to pave the way for the coming of the Messiah. It was inevitable that John's ministry would begin to decrease as Jesus' increased.

Likewise Jesus left his disciples with the promise that the Holy Spirit would come and continue to help them. In some ways they would be even better off with the Holy Spirit in them than they had been with Jesus beside them. The work of the Holy Spirit is to take and apply the saving work of Jesus to all those who would believe.

Paul was great at giving his younger protégés opportunities to serve and lead. They often visited churches in Paul's place in order to encourage them and remind them of the truth. There was never a time when Paul acted in a way that was paranoid or defensive of his ecclesial position. He recognized that they were all on the same team and working towards the same goal.

If you are going to effectively lead your church through the process of succession you have to be willing to loosen your grip on the ball. That might mean letting someone else teach and preach and lead. If this is done with intentionality and purpose it will be a blessing to you, your successor, and the entire congregation. It will happen in a way that is organic and natural.

Pastors who do not know how to decrease make the transition process harder. If you're still preaching 45+ Sundays a year at the age of 64 that might indicate an unwillingness to decrease. I know that everyone loves you and they prefer your preaching, but it is healthy for them to hear from other voices. It's healthy for them to realize that they can survive without you. It's helpful to the pastor-in-training to get some practice.

Vanderbloemen and Bird encourage outgoing pastors to not just share the teaching load, but to also allow potential successors the ability to share the leadership decisions as well. "The goal would be to make sure each of the senior pastor's responsibilities has one or more people who have participated in it enough that they could take over."[50] Allowing others to help share the leadership is not only important training for the successor, it is a healthy practice for the current pastor.

I'm not suggesting that you become lazy or that you stop leading. Instead, intentionally fade back so that the man that you are mentoring has a chance to grow and thrive. You must decrease and he must increase, and that is a good thing.

Don't Abandon Them

Finally, you need to make a commitment from the very beginning of your ministry tenure that you will not abandon the church. A simple rule of thumb is to never leave a place worse than you found it. I don't care what you think God said to you in your last prayer session, you are not "released" from that ministry until you have made sure that they have a leader to take your place. Do not abandon your post!

---

[50] Vanderbloemen and Bird, 35.

It is very hard to follow this rule when you are frustrated or hurt. When you face a rough patch in the ministry, it is tempting to just submit an application to somewhere new and jump ship. Leading your church through a transition is much more complicated when you're unhappy with the church. You might feel that you don't owe them the courtesy or that you've lost the respect required to guide the process.

There's no doubt that there will be times when a pastor has lost all authority and leadership ability in his church. But even if that is the case, you still aren't allowed to simply walk away. Do the necessary work of connecting the church with an outside agent. A third party can help fill the leadership void and guide the church through the next steps.

No matter how angry or hurt you might be, and no matter how ugly and unhealthy the people in the church might be, you still have a responsibility to protect them. Don't act out of spite, but do everything in your power to help the church get to a place of healing and renewal. This also takes a huge amount of humility on your part, but a faithful leader will look past himself and look out for the interests of others.

There are a lot of good reasons why God might call you to a different church. A change in ministry isn't always the result of conflict or failure. Sometimes family issues or ministry abilities necessitate a change. It's something that is good for you and good for the church. If you are sensing that God is calling you on to something different you are not allowed to leave until you lead the church through the transition. You might need to fast track the process, but don't neglect it.

If you are following all the other steps listed above then this one won't be a problem. You have already been praying about it and talking about it with the right people. You've already established an emergency plan. You've already got a leadership pipeline and have been mentoring someone to take the reins. Your church is financially prepared for the shift. Your personal finances are in order. When God calls you to move, it will be a smooth and easy transition.

You are either preparing your church for a successful transition, or you are setting it up for failure. Tossing the keys to the search committee is not a transition plan, it is abandonment. You can do better than that. The church deserves better than that. You're not allowed to leave until you've done everything you can to pass the baton safely to the next pastor.

Stage 2: Navigating through the Transition

The things that a pastor does in the first stage will help pave the way for the second stage in the succession process. In this stage the handoff is imminent. Hopefully, all the people are in place and a date has been set. There are some very important things that the outgoing pastor can do during this time to help ensure a smooth transition.

Set Clear Parameters

A friend of mine took an associate pastor position with the understanding that he would eventually take over as the senior pastor. He was hired because he had a solid education and looked like he would be a good fit as the next pastor. The senior pastor had no intention of abandoning the church and wanted to make sure that the transition was seamless.

The only problem was that the outgoing pastor didn't really want to leave. He wasn't willing to give up many leadership responsibilities. He didn't allow his associate to preach very often. But worst of all he had no departure date set. What looked at first to be a couple of years of training followed by a handoff turned into a mushy "someday." After a couple years it became obvious that a transition was still a long way away. Failure to set clear parameters makes the whole process more frustrating than it needs to be.

In the case of First Baptist Church of Dallas, Pastor Criswell had made promises to his potential successors, but failed to follow through. He kept changing the arrangement. Something more formal than a verbal agreement was necessary. Vanderbloemen and Bird advise, "While contracts are often viewed as needed only in adversarial situations, we believe smart churches will write down agreements about provisions for retirement, intended dates for transition, and other stated intentions about the process."[51]

---

[51] Vanderbloemen & Bird, 109.

You've had plenty of time to prepare for the transition, now it's time to solidify things. Set a date, establish clear transition goals, and then stick to the plan.

Give the Congregation Instructions

When a pastor who is loved and respected leaves it can be a little scary for the congregation. It's an emotional time, but the fear is greatly reduced when they know what to expect next. They will need to hear some words of encouragement and instruction from you before you exit the pulpit.

Let the congregation know that it's natural to be sad about your leaving. When a pastor moves on it is a lot like a death. They love you and know that you love them. It's good to allow time to mourn and process the grief, but that grief should not turn into bitterness or anger toward the new pastor. Let them know that they can be both sad about your leaving and excited about the new pastor coming. It's not an act of disloyalty if they like the new pastor too. In fact, one of the best ways to show respect to you is by graciously welcoming the incoming pastor.

In the two case studies that I conducted there was a stark difference between what was communicated to the churches. My predecessor told the congregation that they were not allowed to call him and complain about me. He said, "If you start to gripe, I will hang up on you." He gave them permission to call him and talk about sports or the weather, but no amount of badmouthing would be tolerated. He emphasized that petty complaining shouldn't happen at all.

In the church that struggled, the outgoing pastor said very little about the transition. It was almost as if he was ignoring the topic. He had no idea who the new pastor would be so he didn't have the ability to say much about him. He failed to give any word of guidance or encouragement.

You know your congregation better than anyone. When the time comes you will know what they need to hear. Don't treat the topic like its taboo. They need to hear from you. They will listen to your instructions. Be open and honest about what's happening, what they can expect, and how they can be a part of making the transition a success.

Celebrate the Hand Off

Resigning or retiring from a church will be more emotionally painful than you think it's going to be. Even under the best of circumstances, it's still hard to say goodbye to people that you love, a routine that you are comfortable with, and a title that has defined you as a person. I haven't met a pastor yet who wasn't bummed out during the process.

It can be tough to celebrate when you don't feel like it. It feels weird and a little insincere to be excited and positive when your heart is breaking. An unhealthy focus on yourself will sour the handoff. Even though there is grief in the change, there is also a lot of joy.

If done right you will have the joy of knowing that the person who is replacing you is a godly man and has a heart of love for the church. You will have invested in him and know that he will be a blessing to the church. You will be able to look ahead with excitement and joy to what God will continue to do through that local congregation.

Hold a special ceremony where you openly celebrate the handoff. Help the rest of the congregation see that the change is something filled will hope, joy, and promise. Remind them that God is totally in control. Encourage them to continue to be a blessing to the new pastor just like they have been to you. Celebrate what God has done all through the years that you have been there and celebrate what He will do in the years ahead.

An important part of celebrating the handoff is to allow the people in your church to honor you as the outgoing pastor. "If you refuse to let people make a big deal of your leaving, you're not doing them a favor; instead, you're depriving them from blessing you and in turn being blessed themselves."[52] Allow people to show you their love for all you have done for them.

Give Your Successor Your Blessing

A central part of celebrating the hand off should involve intentionally giving your successor your blessing. My predecessor didn't give me a leather mantle like Elijah instead he gave me a new sport coat. After preaching his last sermon, which was all about God's guidance and blessing, he took off the coat and put it on me. He prayed over me, blessed me, and commended me to the whole congregation. Just like Moses did with Joshua, I was given a portion of his authority.

Your blessing is no small thing. It is immeasurably valuable. It is a gift that only you can give. You really do have the ability to transfer your authority to the next pastor. As I mentioned earlier, that gift can only be given if you have a relationship with your successor. A genuine blessing flows from a close relationship and a confidence that God is present in the process.

In the book *Next* the authors talk about a concept called Parish Poker. The idea was first suggested by Leith Anderson in an article in Leadership Journal.

> Leith says most pastors start with a positive balance of chips. "When a new pastor is called to a church, a pile of chips is normally stacked up for use as the pastor chooses. They

[52] Vanderbloemen and Bird, 173.

represent the good favor and support of the church people. They may be saved for a rainy day or risked in the first hand of play," he explains.[53]

Just like in the game of poker you will either add to your stack of chips or see them dwindle away. Every new pastor starts with a stack of chips. What he does in the days and months ahead will either cause him to lose or gain more chips. Good sermons, building relationships, wise counseling, and smart stewardship might help a pastor gain chips; bad sermons, inability to relate with people, and traumatic changes will lose him some chips.

Anderson explains how much the predecessor affects the new pastor's chip count:

> Long-term pastors are hard to follow; they often seem to take most of the chips with them. Long-term pastors who died in the church are particularly unfollowable…

> In contrast are those marvelous predecessors who prepare the way. They teach the congregation to love and support the next pastor 'no matter who'. They even make a special point to endorse their successors and thereby confer hundreds (maybe even thousands) of their own chips.[54]

---

[53] Vanderbloemen and Bird, 56.
[54] Vanderbloemen and Bird, 57.

There is value in blessing your successor even if you haven't built a close relationship with him. But the value of a pastoral blessing that comes from a man who everyone recognizes as a mentor to a man that everyone recognizes as the protégé is even greater. The congregation will know that you aren't just politely wishing the new pastor good luck, but that you actually give your blessing to him. Don't be stingy. Give the next leader your blessing.

Get Out of the Way

Finally, after your final sermon has been given, after you've given clear instruction to the congregation, after you have ceremonially passed the baton, after your blessing has been conferred, it's important that you get out of the way. You can't hand your authority over to the new pastor one day and then try to grab it back from him the next.

This isn't a problem if you are leaving to take another ministry positon, but for men who are retiring it can be tough. In chapters 3, 4, and 5 of *Next* the authors share a number of different case studies of pastors who had left well. The key is making sure that you have something to do once you step down. "Having a plan for where outgoing pastors will spend their energy is crucial to a healthy succession."[55]

Some say that the wise thing to do is simply stay away from the church completely for at least a year. Some feel like they can still attend without getting involved. Others might want to stick around and continue to help serve and support the new pastor. I don't know if there is one right way to do things, but there is plenty of anecdotal evidence to suggest that the wisest ting to do is step away for a while.

One of the reasons that disconnecting from the church for a lengthy period of time is wise is that is gives your family some time to disconnect and process the change. In many churches the pastor's wife is heavily involved in all kinds of ministries. She has gained a measure of respect and authority over the years. She is also the strongest supporter and defender of her husband's ministry.

Watching changes take place and things done differently is often harder for your family than it is for you. If your wife remains active once you step down, there is potential for conflict. She needs to have the opportunity to take a step back from service as well. Your family needs to learn how to adjust to life as regular church members. Go visit other churches, take some vacations together, maybe even sleep in once or twice.

> If there is any one "hidden" key to the success or failure of a pastoral succession that we have found, it's the essential role of the outgoing pastor's extended family. Having a serious,

---

[55] Vanderbloemen and Bird, 43.

intentional talk with your family members before your transition is essential. It should cover their roles, their need to step out of the way, their need to support the new pastor, and any financial implications for life after you're no longer the senior pastor.[56]

The old saying about idle hands being the devil's workshop is true even of pastors. It will be much easier for you to get out of the way if you have a specific place to go. "The best succession typically occurs when the outgoing pastor has lined up a new challenge and is excited about what is ahead."[57]

It's not good enough to simply create physical distance; you also have to refrain from any conversations that might detract from the authority of the new pastor. Hold fast to your rule of not allowing anyone to badmouth your successor. Don't jump in and try to fix things. Don't agree to do a funeral without first deferring to the new pastor. Work hard to stay out of the way.

Get out of the way, but don't go too far away. There are still some things you can do to support your successor...from a healthy distance.

---

[56] Vanderbloemen and Bird, 70.
[57] Vanderbloemen and Bird, 56.

Stage 3: Supporting Your Successor

Pastors who leave often settle into one of two extremes that are both unhealthy for the church. Either he will completely disconnect and have absolutely nothing to do with the old church or he will continue to be involved and unintentionally sabotage the transition process. The problem that every outgoing pastor must solve is how much to be involved without crossing over any lines of authority.

You should distance yourself from the congregation and anything that could unintentionally detract from the respect and authority of the new pastor. Your desire is to help him grow into the new role with a minimum of distractions. It will take the congregation some time to see him as the leader. However, there are some things that you can and should do in this phase of the process.

Be Available to the New Pastor

For my first few years as the pastor I made it a point to schedule regular coffee meetings with my predecessor. Even though he had already done a lot to mentor me and teach me, there were still some things that I needed to learn. There are some lessons that only make sense once you are in the midst of regular pastoral leadership.

On more than one occasion I called up the previous pastor and asked him to fill me in on the backstory of someone in the church who was asking for a meeting. He had decades of counseling insight and family history. He was able to give me a healthy perspective about people in the church that enabled me to counsel and encourage them better.

I also found it incredibly valuable to talk through my frustrations with the board, my questions about how to manage the staff, and my ideas about how to update certain programs. As a young man, I tend to be a little less patient and more inclined to just take action. He helped to remind me that God is totally in charge, and encouraged me to wait. So much conflict comes from a lack of understanding of other people and a lack of patience. I had a direct link to someone who could help me understand those unique people.

Once you leave and hand things off to your successor, make sure that you make yourself available to him. Meet with him, answer his questions, point out the pitfalls, offer insight, caution him, cheer him on, and keep supporting him! Even if you move to the other side of the country to take a job at a different church, consider it a part of your ongoing ministry to answer the phone when he calls.

I have no idea how any replacement pastor could succeed without drawing on the insight of the last pastor. There is no doubt in my mind that I would not have survived past my first year without the ongoing help of the previous pastor. He was like a deep well of wisdom and insight that I kept going back to again and again. No one else in the world had the kind of information that he had. I am eternally grateful that he didn't abandon me.

Don't Give People a Place to Criticize

You've already instructed the congregation to not call you to complain about the new pastor, but that won't stop them from doing it anyway. There is a very good chance that people will intentionally seek you out to complain. Maybe it's because they are still a little upset that you left and want to subtly scold you. For some, badmouthing the new pastor is a weird showing of their loyalty to you. Maybe they think you really want to know about what's happening so you can come in and fix it.

Whatever the reason behind the complaining, don't give it a hearing. Shut it down before it even starts. Follow through on your threat to hang up on people if they start talking bad about your successor. Clearly communicate that you are not the right place to sound off. Redirect people to the new pastor so that he can have a fair chance to respond.

Model Grace and Humility

You will have opportunities in the months that follow your departure to model grace and humility and patience for people. You'll have a chance to reaffirm the calling of your successor and your confidence that God will continue to mold and shape him into the man He wants him to be. Keep being a source of encouragement and support.

The things that you do as a leader before, during, and after the succession will play a huge part in the success or failure of the transition. An event this important requires healthy, strong, humble leadership. God has given pastors the huge responsibility of nurturing and caring for the church. Be faithful to honor God by doing everything you can to make sure that the church continues to be a beacon of light long after you are gone.

Chapter 6

A WORD TO THE NEW PASTOR

This book is primarily written to men who are currently serving as senior pastors. My target is pastors who need to see succession planning as a part of their leadership responsibilities as the pastor of the church. But I want to share a few words of wisdom to anyone entering into a new pastoral role. The research shows that there are some simple things that you can do to make sure that the transition is a success.

Honor the Old Pastor

In *The Elephant in the Board Room* principle number one is "Honor thy predecessor." It's very likely that he is someone the people in the church love and respect. It is very common for them to talk about him, and vitally important that you not feel insecure or offended by it when they do. Weese and Crabtree advise, "Practically, honoring our predecessor means we should use TLC with members regarding a predecessor. That's *talk, listen,* and *confirm.*"[58]

---

[58] Weese and Crabtree, 16.

When someone says, "The last pastor was such a great preacher!" There is a natural inclination to take those words as a jab at your preaching ability. They must be trying to say that you stink. They are unfairly comparing you with him! That's not right! That's not fair! He wasn't that great of a preacher anyway! How dare they! We might react in a way that is defensive or even angry. This communicates to people that they are not allowed to even talk about the last pastor in your presence.

It's possible that they are taking a jab at your preaching, especially if you really aren't as good as the last preacher. But they might just be expressing the fact that they miss him. It might not really be about you. Let them talk, listen to them, and then confirm their words. An appropriate response might be to say, "You are right. I hope to one day be as good as he is!" It's okay to join people as they acknowledge the huge contribution that the last pastor had in their lives.

Vanderbloemen and Bird point out, "Seamless transitions are rare, but they do happen, even in extreme circumstances. Most of the time the seamlessness can be traced back to a key principle: when the past is honored, future possibilities are unlocked."[59] Don't overlook the importance of showing respect to past leaders and past ministries.

This will be so much easier for you to do if you already have a close relationship with your predecessor. It will be easy for you to honor him in public because you genuinely respect him. Honoring

---

[59] Vanderbloemen and Bird, 175.

your predecessor is also easier when you are more concerned with humbly loving other people than you are with protecting your ego.

I made it a point to let the whole church know that I was still regularly meeting with the last pastor. I thanked him publically for his wisdom and guidance. I made it safe for other people to talk about how much they appreciate him. I joined with the congregation in their shared appreciation for all that he had done to bless the church over the years.

I also honored my predecessor by seeking out his advice. He did his part by making himself available to me, and I took full advantage of his wisdom. I not only sought out his advice, but I also took it. I trusted him. I listened to him. I still made a few changes and did some things my own way, but I knew that he understood the church better than I did and that he had my best interests in mind. It wasn't hard to trust him.

Frankly, I don't understand why anyone would dishonor their predecessor. Even if he wasn't universally loved by all, it still doesn't make any sense to debase him in some sad attempt to build yourself up as the leader. Ignoring or degrading the man who was there before you is a recipe for disaster.

In my case study of FBC, the new pastor who took over had no contact with the previous pastor. He never sought out his wisdom. He didn't seem to care at all about the nearly 20 years of experience his predecessor had at that church. But what was worse, the new pastor began to openly criticize the theology of the previous pastor.

His failure to honor his predecessor was one of the reasons he lasted less than two years.

Don't make that same mistake. Go out of your way to let people talk about their beloved former pastor. Listen to what they have to say with humility, and recognize that it probably isn't a criticism of you as much as it is their way of honoring him. And then, instead of scolding them or refuting them, confirm their words. Join people as they honor him, and then honor him yourself by seeking out his wisdom.

Go Slow

The advice to take things slow, especially at first, is so obvious that it almost seems unnecessary to mention. But no matter how often this advice is given, people still fail to heed it. We don't go slowly. We don't want to wait. We can't wait to get right to work fixing all the problems and cleaning up the mess. We enter into the church with excitement and anticipation. There are so many great things that God has for us to do, and we want to get them all done by the end of our first week.

One of the main reasons that so many churches experience conflict and trauma after a pastoral transition is because the new leader doesn't take the time to understand how things work before he starts to make changes. He doesn't take the time to build relationships before he starts expecting people to respect his new ideas. He comes across as someone who is very dishonoring to the predecessor because he wants to dismantle the things that the former pastor established.

The advice to go slow isn't just for men who are young and new. Even if you've been a pastor for 20 years and are just changing churches, still go slow! Even if you have a history of success, still go slow! Even if it seems like everyone is telling you to go fast, still go slow!

Build relationships first. Learn why things are the way they are first. Build up enough trust so that people will understand that changes are not an attack on the previous pastor but a natural part of moving forward. That process takes a lot of time. Be patient.

Keep Learning

When I took over as the senior pastor I was young and green. I asked the congregation to be patient with me as I developed. I promised them that, if they hung with me, I would work hard at becoming a better preacher and a better leader and a better pastor. I vowed to them that I would do my part to become the pastor that they deserved, and I invited them to be a part of the process of training me. I gave them permission to offer advice and feedback. I encouraged them to come and tell me when I screwed up.

The people in my church totally kept their end of the bargain. They suffered patiently through bad sermons, gently rebuked me when I said dumb things, and gave me extra room to grow. They never expected perfection, but instead saw me as someone who needed their love and support.

But I had to keep my end of the deal. I read books and took classes on how to preach better. I practiced a lot. I sought out advice and wisdom from more experienced pastors. I worked hard at memorizing names. I built relationships with people. I prayed daily for God to grow me.

As a result, my whole church gets the credit for my growth and development as a pastor. They weren't just passive observers, but active participants with me. People will regularly comment on how much I've grown since I started, and I make sure to thank them for helping with that process. I also encourage them to keep up the good work because I still have a lot left to learn!

I've had a safe place to learn and grow, but if I didn't do anything to improve, at some point the patience and good will of the people in my church would have run out. Just because I had a couple of degrees and the title of pastor didn't mean that I was done learning. In a lot of ways my education was just beginning.

Strive every day to improve. Don't ever get to the place where you think you have arrived as a pastor. There will always be areas for growth as God shapes you into the leader that He wants you to be.

CONCLUSION

The kind of arthritis that I was diagnosed with attacks the lower back and often causes the vertebrate to fuse together. It flared up in my hips, back, and neck. When it was at its worst it was hard for me to move at all. All I wanted to do was stay in bed. I was shocked to learn that the best treatment is exercise. Movement helps to prevent bone fusion and it helps to relieve the pain. It seemed so counter-intuitive, but my doctor encouraged me to move more!

At first, exercising with a sore back was hard to do! But I knew that failure to get moving would only make the arthritis pain worse and ultimately lead to permanent disability. I started slow with swimming and low impact exercises. Eventually I added in some weight lifting. It took time, but I felt better and better every week!

It can be a little uncomfortable, maybe even painful, to talk about succession. Maybe it seems counter-intuitive to think of leadership transition as a part of maintaining church health. But as you move the conversation forward you will begin to see your church grow stronger and help to ensure long term health.

My primary goal in writing this book is to encourage pastors to begin the conversation about their own eventual departure. Succession planning is an important part of your responsibility as the pastor. As the God-appointed leader of your church your job is not to merely build up ministries and programs, but to build up the next generation of leaders.

John Maxwell reminds leaders, "Achievement comes to someone when he is able to do great things for himself. Success comes when he empowers followers to do great things *with* him. Significance comes when he develops leaders to do great things *for* him. But a legacy is created only when a person puts his organization into a position to do great things *without* him."[60] As pastors our role is far greater than simply attaining a measure of personal and professional success. We need to look beyond ourselves and look forward to creating a long-term legacy of church health.

We are not called to individual achievement, or personal success, or even the comfort of significance, we are called to maintain the legacy of the church. The high calling of pastoral ministry demands leaders like Moses and Elijah and Paul, who are willing to humbly decrease so that the next generation of leaders can take over.

Vanderbloemen and Bird point out,

Good pastors focus their life on producing good fruit. But the greatest and most visionary pastors and church leaders share a common wisdom: they plan not just for their current 'tree' but also for the time beyond their own tenure.

---

[60] John Maxwell, *The 21 Irrefutable Laws of Leadership: Follow Them and People Will Follow You.* (Nashville, TN: Thomas Nelson, 1998.), 221

What would happen if that wisdom and vision were talked about among church leaders from day one of their tenure? What if seminaries and pastoral internships made 'Securing Your Legacy' a required course? What could happen?

If the culture changed, the exception of good succession planning might become the rule. The change would lead to a healthier church overall.[61]

I understand that what I am advocating for here in this book is not a minor adjustment, but a cultural change within the church world. This kind of shift might not happen immediately, but as we talk about succession and pray about succession and learn about succession it will slowly become a normal part of pastoral leadership. I firmly believe that good succession planning can become the rule and not the exception!

As I was finishing up this study in the summer of 2015 a book titled *Seamless Succession: Simplifying Church Leadership Transitions* was published. In the forward, written by Jim Tomberlin he says, "Pastoral succession has been a neglected topic in the church but is finally coming out of the closet. The majority of churches today are being led by aging baby-boomers. There is a tsunami of senior pastoral transitions coming over the next decade as

---

[61] Vanderbloemen and Bird, 179.

these aging baby-boomers retire. Most will not be ready out of fear or uncertainty on how to start the succession conversation."[62]

Many pastors won't be ready because they didn't know they were supposed to get ready. But as I've shown in the first part of this book, the old idea that succession planning was not the pastor's job is an unhealthy, outdated, and unbiblical idea. During a time of transition good leadership is more important than ever!

God's word gives us great examples of leaders who went to great lengths to pass on their knowledge of God to the next generation. They understood how valuable and important it is to make sure that the word of God and the church of God is preserved. We only looked at three examples, but the Bible is full of people who paved the way for their replacements.

My challenge to you is to start the conversation. If you are a pastor, start talking to your family and your board. Keep reading about this topic. Keep thinking about how to best transition at your church. Don't wait for someone else to take the lead here, you are the one that God has called to lead!

If you are a denominational leader or someone who has the privilege of interacting with pastors, let me encourage you to help pastors think through this process. It's time to abandon the notion that succession should be left up to a regional office or a search committee. Help pastors be better leaders. Provide them with

---

[62] Passavant , *iv.*

resources to begin working on a plan of succession. Help their church financially prepare. I believe that assisting pastors in this area is one of the most important things that a denomination can do for its churches.

More than anything else I would encourage you as the pastor to move forward with humility and grace. The thought of leaving your church is painful, but God can and will make the whole process a blessing. May God's grace fall on you and every man who follows you!

Appendix

TWO CASE STUDIES

The book <u>Next</u> by William Vanderbloemen and Warren Bird contains some of the most helpful case studies on pastoral transitions. They have investigated and documented the details surrounding the process of succession at dozens of churches. Some of the transitions went well and some went poorly. Almost all of their examples are from large, prominent churches. The two case studies that I offer here are from smaller, rural churches.

It is difficult to diagnose problems in the church and offer solutions because every church is unique. There are a million variables that contribute to the health and life of each and every church. The size, geographic location, denomination, history, ethnicity, social status, building type, and carpet color are just a few of the different factors. No two churches are alike.

In an effort to strip away some of the differences I've chosen two churches that have a lot in common. Both churches are in the same small town, with approximately the same weekly attendance. They are both Baptist in affiliation, and both had well-loved pastors with lengthy tenures. But even with the similarities, one of the churches experienced a seamless transition (my church, obviously) and the other church struggled.

Case Study #1:
First Baptist Church

This case study was compiled from a series of interviews with the current pastor, a former pastor, a former board member, and a former member of the church. Since this case study involves the church that I grew up in and have remained close with I am also able to offer my own first-hand experience.

First Baptist Church (FBC) has had a long and prestigious presence in the community. It was one of the first churches to be established in the town. Over the years the FBC had gone through the normal ups and downs of church life. It was a church that had experienced good and bad leadership, times of peace and times of conflict, and normal cycles of growth. Through every phase it remained faithful to the core mission of sharing the gospel.

In the early 1990's FBC was entering into a time of unprecedented growth. Weekly attendance was between 400-500, giving was strong, and the ministries were thriving. There were a lot of young families and there was a feeling of life and energy at the church. It was the most prominent church in town.

I interviewed one former staff member who said, "Ministry was fun during those years. Everything just clicked. Lots of young families were showing up every week. It was great!"

Pastor Robert Smith[63] was a caring pastor who led the church well, supported by a team of pastors who all served faithfully. The gospel was being proclaimed and new people were coming to faith in Christ. The church enjoyed over a decade of growth.

Things began to shift in the early 2000's. A number of events took place that started to erode the foundation and set the church up for a decade that would be marked by decline. Many of the shifts were directly and indirectly related to the fact that Pastor Smith was getting closer to retiring.

In 2002 the worship pastor was given the green light to start up a Saturday evening worship service. The purpose was to help relieve a little of the congestion on Sunday mornings, but it was also designed to be a more contemporary worship experience. The worship pastor took on the responsibilities of leading the music and preaching at these services. It didn't take long before that Saturday night service had grown to over 100 people.

When Pastor Smith announced his intention to retire in 2004 the worship pastor made it known that he wanted to be the successor. The staff member I spoke with shared that the worship pastor

---

[63] Some of the names in this case study have been changed out of respect for all involved.

believed he had been promised the position. His understanding was that the senior pastor had been using the Saturday evening service to prepare him.

The problem was that Pastor Smith had no recollection of promising the position to the worship pastor, or anyone else. In addition, the rest of the staff and the church board didn't think he was the best fit. The former staff member explained that a rift had grown between the worship pastor and the rest of the pastoral staff. "He began to become more autonomous and independent. Things had become tense in the staff meetings."

According to one man who was a board member during that time the entire board felt that hiring any one of the associate pastors would make things too political and cause a church split. It was their intention to look for someone from the outside.

I asked the former staff member if Pastor Smith had done anything to prepare the church or the board or the staff for his retirement. He replied, "Not much. He gave us a retirement date and let the search committee take over from there." The church constitution made it clear that the elder board was responsible for finding a replacement. So setting a retirement date and handing things off to the board was all that was expected of the pastor.

There had been no real discussion of what would happen when the pastor retired. No leadership pipeline had been established. No one had been identified or trained to take over. Pastor Smith had absolutely no reason to plan for his departure or work towards equipping a successor. That just wasn't how things were done. He followed the normal process for pastoral succession.

Pastor Smith made it clear that he would not recommend the worship pastor to be his replacement. And the board made it clear that they would be looking for someone from the outside and not considering any internal candidates. As a result the worship pastor eventually left to start his own church on the other side of town. He took with him most of the people who were a part of the Saturday evening service. It had essentially been a smaller church within a bigger church and so the split was not a surprise.

Despite the setback, FBC continued to move forward with excitement and hope. The board member I spoke with viewed the departure of the worship pastor as a relatively minor setback. Sunday mornings were still well attended and there was still a lot of energy. He was excited about bringing in a new pastor and felt that it would help the church grow even more.

The elder board selected a search committee that got right to work weeding through the stack of applications and praying about who the next pastor would be. The search committee was made up primarily of current and past board members, all men. The senior pastor was not a part of that team and neither was any of the staff. All of the men on the search committee were chosen because they were faithful men of God who were actively involved and had a deep love for the church. They all entered into the task with careful attention.

In 2005, after a yearlong search process, Pastor Dave Jones was called to replace Pastor Smith. Pastor Jones had a solid education and had served well in other ministry positions. He was a good theologian and a gifted preacher. Pastor Smith was not a bad preacher, but the hope was that Pastor Jones would be able to bring even more energy and theological clarity to the pulpit.

After a ceremonial goodbye to Pastor Smith the new man jumped right into action. There was very little down time between the retirement of Pastor Smith and the hiring of Pastor Jones. The people in the church were excited to move forward, and Pastor Jones was eager to get to work. The future of FBC looked good.

The staff was the first to see the signs that Pastor Jones might not be the right fit. Within the first few months it became evident that his theology leaned more towards hard-line Calvinism. The church had been led for decades by a man who didn't really focus on the theological fine points and tended to be more Arminian in his preaching.

The former staff member that I interviewed said, "I can remember him making an offhand comment in the office one day about Arminians and realizing that there might be a problem." He and other members of the staff tried to warn Pastor Jones that pushing a Calvinistic theology from the pulpit too soon might be met with confusion or even opposition.

The rest of the congregation began to notice that something wasn't quite right when, after a number of months, Pastor Jones still seemed to be distant and disconnected. I spoke with a former member who said that it was hard to talk to Pastor Jones and they often walked away feeling like he didn't care about them. The relational disconnection was also felt from the pulpit. Pastor Smith was always so warm and friendly, and always had a big smile. But Pastor Jones seemed grumpier and angrier. One member said, "His sermons made me feel like I was being scolded."

Unfortunately Pastor Jones didn't take the advice of the staff and the relational gap with the congregation widened. Within six months it became increasingly noticeable that people were leaving and giving was decreasing. After a year, members of the staff began to plan their exit strategies. After another nine months of increasingly heated conflict, Pastor Jones resigned from FBC.

Pastor Jones left feeling like he had been misled. In a parting letter that he wrote to the church he indicated that he had simply done what the search committee had hired him to do. The former pastor explained that a number of the men on the search committee subscribed to a hard Calvinistic theology and wanted that for their next pastor. Either they didn't understand the past theological position of the church, or they wanted to change it. So Pastor Jones was hired with the impression that the church wanted a strong Calvinist preacher. He hadn't been hired to be everyone's friend, but to whip them into theological shape. He was just doing what the search committee had encouraged him to do.

By the time Pastor Jones left, the church had shrunk from about 350 to 200 in attendance. Giving was significantly down and the church incurred more debt. Not only did the church face a decrease in attendance and giving, but a decrease in the size and effectiveness of its ministries. Instead of two years of added growth, those two years were a major setback.

Again, even in spite of the setback, FBC was optimistic about the future. The board member described how they all felt that the problem was just a bad fit and with Pastor Jones gone they would be back on track quickly. Another search committee was assembled and they went to work to find their next pastor. This time they understood the value of having a pastor who was warm and relational. The committee set out to find a leader who was not like Pastor Jones.

The search committee narrowed the field down to two great candidates. They both looked good on paper and their preaching sounded strong. One of them was a younger man who was fresh out of seminary; but ultimately they selected an older man who had a doctorate in church growth and more years of experience. They felt that he would be better at connecting with people and better at helping the church grow. In 2006 Steve Campbell was hired as the next pastor.

Pastor Campbell started strong. He wore Hawaiian shirts and was much more casual and relaxed. He made it a point to connect with different groups in the church. His preaching was far lighter and less condemning than Pastor Jones's had seemed. He even had a big smile that reminded people of Pastor Smith. It seemed like FBC was finally on the road to recovery.

However, Pastor Campbell didn't last much longer than Pastor Jones did. There were a number of factors that led to his eventual resignation. Pastor Campbell wanted to make a lot of changes; many of the changes were too big and too fast. He felt that his mandate was to make FBC a mega-church. I spoke with a member who said they began to feel like they were just tools he was using to help him build his kingdom. He spent a lot of money and accrued a lot more debt, but the church never grew.

Whenever anyone challenged or questioned Pastor Campbell he responded with lengthy and scathing e-mails. More and more people in the church began to see a disturbing side to his leadership. Eventually it was a binder full of those e-mails and the impending financial collapse that helped the church get rid of him. He had served for just over two years.

By this point the church was very close to death. Attendance was down to around 100 people. The debt was huge. Those who had stayed at the church were emotionally winded. The remaining leaders at the church began to talk to another church in town about the possibility of merging. This was the low point.

This time, instead of assembling a search committee the church brought on an interim pastor who could help buy them some time as they regrouped and healed. The board member said that he felt a little gun shy and didn't want to rush into hiring another pastor. The man they brought in wasn't flashy, but he provided stability. One member commented to me, "I finally felt safe going to church again." The interim stayed on for over a year.

During that time the youth pastor had more and more opportunities to preach and teach. He had survived the painful failure of Pastor Campbell and continued to serve the church faithfully. Even though he was young, the members of the church saw his passion for preaching and his love for them and the community. The board began to slowly transition Pastor Cody into the role of senior pastor by allowing him to preach more and giving him greater responsibility for the day-to-day administration of the church.

In 2012 Pastor Cody Cannon took over as the next senior pastor of FBC. In the years that followed Pastor Cody has worked hard to deepen his relationships with the people. Even though he is young, the congregation has been patient and gracious with him as he learns and grows. He did his part to further his education and improve as a preacher and pastor. And as a result he has grown and the church has grown.

Pastor Cody commented to me, "I feel honored and consistently humbled to be a part of what God is doing in our church. He has brought a lot of healing over the last few years and it is incredible to see Him rebuilding a people for His glory despite many man-made mistakes in our recent past."

As of today FBC is a healthy, debt-free, thriving church again. Attendance is back up above 300 and continues to grow. God is an awesome, sovereign God and He used those hard years to help shape His church into something even better and stronger.

There were a number of things that contributed to the failed attempts at replacing Pastor Smith. The problems weren't at all uncommon. They made some of the same mistakes that thousands of other churches make as they attempt to use the same old playbook. The problem isn't that FBC did things horribly wrong; in fact, they did things precisely by the book. The problem is that the book is broken.

The second case study is of a church that made some substantial variations to that old play book, and had very different results.

Case Study #2:
Calvary Baptist Church

This case study involves the church that I am currently pastoring. I was involved with a large part of the process, but I have interviewed the former senior pastor, the youth pastor, and members of the search committee in an effort to better understand the events that led up to my being hired.

In 1969 Pastor Henry Tucker became the pastor of Calvary Baptist Church at the age of 28. For the next 35 years the church saw modest, but consistent growth. Under Pastor Tucker's leadership the church was very stable and healthy. It had a family focus, vibrant ministries, and solid preaching.

I asked Pastor Tucker when he started to think about retirement. He said, "Somewhere around age 55. I'm a planner!" He chose age 65 as his retirement age because he said he had seen too many men who had hung on far too long and he didn't want to be guilty of that himself.

At age 55 he had already been serving at Calvary for almost 30 years. He still had a passion for preaching and a love of ministering to people, but the daily grind of administrative duties was wearing on him. He told me that he had less patience for board meetings and business. He knew that those things were important parts of pastoral leadership. The job isn't just preaching on Sundays; a good pastor has to be able to handle the politics and details of running a church responsibly.

Over the course of the next 10 years Pastor Tucker let the board and his staff know that he intended to retire at age 65. A few years before 65, Pastor Tucker encouraged the board to shift into a more active phase of the transition process. A search committee needed to be formed, a budget needed to be established. They spent time discussing what they would be looking for in their next pastor.

Pastor Tucker consulted a number of different books on the subject of transitions and he contacted the regional representative for the Conservative Baptist Association. Pastor Tucker said that he was encouraged to have very little involvement in the transition process. The rule of thumb then was to allow the church to decide what it wanted next in a pastor. He was told that the best thing for the church was for him to just step away.

Acting on that advice, Pastor Tucker made sure that the board had a good head start, and then he turned the search process over to them. The board went to work assembling a separate search committee and beginning the process of looking for the man that would be the next pastor. The search committee was made up of seven men and women of different ages that represented different demographics. It also contained a member of the board and a member of the staff. In early 2006 the search committee went to work.

Even though Pastor Tucker was not a part of the search process, he still understood that there were some things that only he could do to prepare the congregation for the transition. Pastor Tucker let everyone in the church know about his planned departure a couple of years in advance. He shared with me that he had some reservations about telling people of his retirement, but felt that the more time they had to process the change the healthier it would be.

The advance warning gave people time to grieve and say goodbye and mentally prepare for a change. It also gave Pastor Tucker the freedom to set the stage for the new leader in some important ways. I asked him what he had done during that time to help pave the way for his replacement. He said he spent a lot of time in prayer, he encouraged the congregation to be patient and gracious, and he set some ground rules for them to follow.

Over the next few years as Pastor Tucker preached about patience and forgiveness and grace he reminded the people that they would need to show an extra measure of patience and forgiveness and grace to the new pastor when he came. He took every opportunity to remind people that it was their job to welcome him in and make sure he was cared for and loved. The subject of his departure was a sad thing, but he didn't ignore it, avoid it, or pretend it wasn't really happening.

Pastor Tucker was a little worried that announcing his retirement would make him a lame duck, but just the opposite happened. He discovered a new freedom in his preaching and a renewed confidence. "What are they going to do, fire me?" he joked. The respect that he had earned over 35 years wasn't diminished at all. He was able to effectively use his last few years to slowly shepherd the people to the point that they were spiritually ready to handle a transition.

Even though the rule of thumb said that the old pastor should stay out of the search process, the search committee asked for his advice. On two separate occasions Pastor Tucker was invited in to help guide them. At the beginning of the search process he was called in to help make sure that they were on the right track and had the right information. The members of the search committee that I interviewed said that they wanted to make sure that they hadn't overlooked anything important. They respected and valued Pastor Tucker's wisdom. And at the end of the search they invited him in one more time to ask his opinion about one of the final candidates - me.

In the summer of 2005, just as the board of Calvary Baptist was starting the process of preparing to replace Pastor Tucker, I came to the church. I had just graduated from Western Seminary and had spent months trying to land my first ministry position. Every door had closed on me, so I took a teaching position at Woodland Christian High School in order to feed my family while I continued to look for a church job.

Calvary was the church that my wife had grown up in, and over the years when we had visited home we usually attended church there. So when we moved back it was the most natural place for us to settle. I didn't know at that time that Pastor Tucker was intending to retire and I didn't have any intention of serving as the pastor there. But I was applying for every vacant pastoral position that I could find.

When I showed up Pastor Tucker saw the value of free labor. He put me right to work teaching and filling the pulpit for him. Over the years I had benefited greatly from some amazing pastors who had mentored me and invested in me. Pastor Tucker was a fountain of wisdom, but also just fun to hang out with. I hung close and soaked in as much as I could. He prayed for me, advised me, critiqued my sermons, gave me insight into how to deal with people, and modeled patience and love.

A little less than a year from the time I came to Calvary I learned that Henry was going to retire at age 65. I can remember going into his office and asking him if I should apply. Most of the churches that I was applying to were for youth or associate positions. Even though I didn't really want to work my way up the ministry ladder, I knew that I needed more experience before I'd be hired as a senior pastor. I wasn't sure that Calvary would even consider me because of my young age and relative lack of experience.

Pastor Henry didn't sugar coat things; he let me know that I would be a long shot and that I didn't meet some of the requirements that the search committee had in place. But he also encouraged me to give it a shot. So I filled out the application and submitted it and prayed for God to guide the whole thing.

Almost a year later the search committee called Pastor Tucker to advise them for a second time. This time it was to ask him if they should continue to consider someone young for the positon. By that point the search committee had sifted through a stack of applicants and narrowed things down to just three men. Pastor Tucker broke the "no involvement in the process" rule and met with them.

I asked Pastor Henry, "What did you tell the search committee in that meeting?" He explained that he didn't apply any pressure to the search committee one way or the other. He didn't tell them what to do. He simply reminded them of his own ministry experience.

He had started as the pastor of Calvary at the age of 28, younger than I was. He also had very little experience and not as much seminary training. Even though the search committee guidelines stated that the next pastor needed to have at least five years of experience, Pastor Tucker reminded the search committee that I did have unpaid experience and over a year of experience serving at Calvary. He also reminded the search committee that the people at Calvary were very gracious and loving and would be willing to give me time to grow, just like they had with him.

The members of the search committee that I interviewed both said that the perspective that Pastor Tucker provided helped to encourage them to keep me on the list. The search committee had committed the whole process to prayer and fasting. They followed their guidelines, but not in a way that prevented God from moving in a different direction. The chairman of the search committee commented that they wanted to make sure that they were following God's lead. Their flexibility and openness took them in a direction that they might not have expected, but one that gave them confidence that God was at work.

In the end it came down to just two people - me and a man I had gone to seminary with. Both similar in age and experience, and both a good fit for the church. They didn't want to simply hire me because I was the known quantity so they went back to God again and asked for His clear guidance. God responded by allowing the other candidate to receive a call to a different church, leaving the search committee with just one name left.

I was recommended to the congregation who voted to approve me with a 98% majority! I officially took over for Pastor Tucker on January 1, 2007. There was a transition service where Pastor Tucker passed the mantle to me, in the form of a sport coat. In front of the whole congregation he affirmed me and commissioned me and blessed me. Then he again charged the congregation to be patient and gracious with me. He told them that if anyone called him to complain he would hang up on them. After the service he gave out some hugs, said goodbye, and then left.

He wouldn't return to regular attendance at Calvary for more than a year. That was by design. He wanted to give me time to be seen as the leader. He read the advice of Bob Russell in *When God Builds a Church*, "I have watched closely and have yet to see a retired minister remain in the church he pastored for a long time and not be a burden to his successor. It's too great a temptation."[64] So Pastor Tucker stayed away.

Even though he stayed away from the church, he didn't abandon me. We continued to meet on a regular basis. At that point I still had a ton that I needed to learn. He listened to my struggles and offered balanced, informed advice. He encouraged me to slow down and take my time. He explained to me the history of some of the tough cases in the church. He pointed out the major land mines that I should avoid. He prayed for me. His guidance in those first few years was invaluable!

Pastor Tucker had prayed that after he retired God would grant him the opportunity to mentor some young men in the ministry and help build them up. God answered that prayer in an amazing way. He was able to build up the man who would ultimately take his

---

[64] Bob Russell and Rusty Russell, *When God Builds a Church: 10 Principles for Growing a Dynamic Church: The Remarkable Story of Southeast Christian Church* (West Monroe, LA: Howard Publishing, 2000), 89.

place, just like Moses with Joshua or Elijah with Elisha. His ministry influence didn't end when he turned 65, it just shifted.

Almost nine years later I am still serving at Calvary Baptist Church. I hope to be here for the next 25! I not only survived following a long-term pastor, but I've thrived because of it. I've been blessed in countless ways by the things that Pastor Tucker did before, during, and after the transition. I'm striving every day to honor him and become deserving of the position that God has called me to. Looking back I have no doubt in my mind that any success I've experienced has more to do with what Pastor Tucker did for me than what I have done.

Comparing and Contrasting the Two Case Studies

Both of these Baptist churches were in the same town, with a similar cultural setting, both about the same size, both with pastors who had served for a long time; yet the outcome was very different. What happened that led to success in one case and failure in the other? There are some definite differences that might help us gain better insight into how a transition should take place.

First, it's important to note that both Pastor Smith and Pastor Tucker fully bought into the idea that the pastor was not supposed to have any involvement in their succession. They both were told that they should set a date, have the board establish a search committee, and then just get out of the way. Both of them followed that rule because they wholeheartedly loved their church and wanted what was best.

The difference is that one of the two pastors broke the rules. Pastor Henry didn't just set a retirement date and then fade away. He talked about his departure. He preached about unity and grace. He comforted the fears of people. He did everything he could to help set the table for the next man. The amount of discussion about the pending transition from Pastor Smith was much more limited.

Pastor Henry also met with the search committee, even though that was against the rules. The committee knew that Pastor Tucker wanted to have a very limited involvement, but they respected his opinion and guidance enough to call him for help anyway. They realized that he had access to some information and knowledge that no one else did. And even though he wasn't supposed to, Pastor Tucker willingly met with the committee. Even though it was a limited contact, Pastor Tucker was able to provide a level of wisdom and leadership that the committee needed to be able to make an informed decision.

Pastor Tucker also didn't follow the advice of those who said he should keep his distance. He stayed away from church, but he didn't abandon me. He was always right there for me whenever I needed him. He didn't have to spend as much time and energy working with me for all those years. He had earned the right to spend his days at a nice trout stream. But like Paul writing to encourage Timothy in his

163

first ministry appointment, Pastor Tucker kept teaching me through my first ministry appointment.

There were also some very significant differences in the two search committees. At FBC the committee was made up of a group of men who all shared a Calvinistic theological slant. The problem was that their view was a minority in that church. Instead of a search committee made up of a cross-section of different people from within the church, their committee was biased in one direction.

There's a good possibility that their theological preferences guided their process and led to the outcome. The man they hired was a strong five point Calvinist and a good preacher, but not very relational or gentle. The lopsided search committee didn't represent the church as a whole. They didn't understand the theological makeup of the people in the church. The new pastor came with the understanding that it was a Calvinistic church that was looking for some solid Calvinistic preaching. He had been set up to fail.

At no point in the process was Pastor Smith consulted. As the theological leader of the church he would have been able to advise against hiring a man like Pastor Jones, but he never had the opportunity. It wasn't due to any error on his part. Pastor Smith was simply following the rules. He wasn't supposed to be involved.

Not only was Pastor Smith not involved with the search process, but no member of the staff was on the committee! The men who had been leading and loving the people in that church for decades were not a part of guiding the process. Their advice likely would not have been heeded, but they never had a chance to offer it.

Pastor Smith had no relationship with Pastor Jones and no way to pass on to him any authority or blessing. He didn't know him, and likely would not have chosen him for the job. The handoff was merely positional. Pastor Smith also didn't leave the church. He was often serving at other churches on Sunday morning, but when he was in town he continued to attend FBC. When people called him to complain about the new pastor he deflected for as long as he could, but at some point his disappointment and frustration began to show through.

As I interviewed different people who had gone through the traumatic transition at FBC, they all point to an underlying attitude of entitlement and pride that permeated the church. They were a church that had doctors and judges and senators in attendance. They had a growing attendance. They were the hip, sophisticated church. They deserved someone with a high level of prestige as their pastor. There's no way that they would have ever considered a kid right out of school.

Looking back it's really hard to assign blame to anyone. Pastor Smith didn't do anything wrong. He was simply following the guidelines that he was given. The board had some obvious weaknesses, but the man they hired could have succeeded. Pastor

Jones was just doing what he thought the church wanted him to do. Calvary was playing with the exact same rule book.

The key difference is that Calvary broke the rules. Pastor Tucker didn't stick to the notion that he couldn't help out the search committee. The committee didn't slavishly stick to their written guidelines. Pastor Tucker continued to help me out even after I took over. I think that if Calvary had followed those old rules of transitions the outcome would have likely been very similar to FBC.

That's why I wrote this. To encourage pastors to break the old rules. Instead, with prayer and humility and patience, develop a transition plan that makes the most sense for your context. The new rule of thumb is simply to not be afraid to take the lead. The methods you use to find and train and transition to the new man might be different, but pastor, your leadership is key!

Secular Succession

Bennis, Warren G. Why Leaders Can't Lead: The Unconscious Conspiracy Continues. San Francisco: Jossey-Bass, 1989.

Carey, Dennis C., and Dayton Ogden. *CEO Succession.* Oxford UK: Oxford UP, 2000.

Charan, Ram, Stephen J. Drotter, and James L. Noel. *The Leadership Pipeline: How to Build the Leadership Powered Company.* San Francisco: Jossey-Bass, 2011.

Collins, James C. *Good to Great and the Social Sectors: Why Business Thinking Is Not the Answer : A Monograph to Accompany Good to Great : Why Some Companies Make the Leap--and Others Don't.* Boulder, Colo.: J. Collins, 2005.

-------------------_____. *Good to Great: Why Some Companies Make the Leap--and Others Don't.* New York, NY: HarperBusiness, 2001.

Drucker, Peter F. *The Effective Executive.* New York: Harper & Row, 1967.

Maxwell, John C. The 21 Irrefutable Laws of Leadership: Follow Them and People Will Follow You. Nashville, TN: Thomas Nelson, 1998.

Rothwell, William J. *Effective Succession Planning: Ensuring Leadership Continuity and Building Talent from within.* New York: AMACOM, American Management Association, 2005.

Wolfe, Rebecca Luhn. *Systematic Succession Planning: Building Leadership from Within.* Menlo Park, CA: Crisp Publications, 1996.

Web Articles and Research Studies

Arn, Charles. "Pastoral Longevity and Church Growth," *Wesleyconnectonline.com*, <http://wesleyconnectonline.com/pastoral-longevity-and-church-growth-charles-arn/> (Accessed June 10, 2015).

Cooper, Steve. "Look For Employees with High EQ Over IQ." *Forbes.com,* <http://www.forbes.com/sites/stevecooper/2013/03/18/look-for-employees-with-high-eq-over-iq/> (Accessed June 10, 2015).

Dever, Mark. "What's Wrong With Search Committees?" *9Marks.com* <http://9marks.org/article/whats-wrong-search-committees-part-1-2-finding-pastor/> (Accessed February 4, 2016).

Green, Lisa Cannon. "Former Pastors Report Lack of Support Led to Abandoning Pastorate" *Lifeway Research,* <http://www.lifewayresearch.com/2016/01/12/former-pastors-report-lack-of-support-led-to-abandoning-pastorate/> (Accessed January 12, 2016).

Hartford Institute for Religious Research. "What's the Average Size of US Churches?" <> (Accessed July 10, 2015).

Kamenetz, Anya. "The Four-Year Career," *Fastcompany.com*, <http://www.fastcompany.com/1802731/four-year-career> (Accessed December 12, 2015).

Korn, Melissa, "Is It Better to Promote From Within?" *Wall Street Journal* http://www.wsj.com/articles/SB10001424052702304750404577320000041035504> (Accessed July 10, 2015).

Krejcir, Richard J. "Statistics on Pastors" *Into the Word* *http://www.intothyword.org/apps/articles/?articleid=36562*(Accessed June 4, 2015).

McGregor, Jena. "The Rate of CEO Change," *Washingtonpost.com*, <https://www.washingtonpost.com/national/on-leadership/the-rate-of-ceo-turnover/2012/05/24/gJQAJrAMnU_story.html> (Accessed June 24, 2015).

Miles, Stephen A. "Succession Planning: How To Do It Right", *Forbes.com*, <http://www.forbes.com/2009/07/31/succession-planning-right-leadership-governance-ceos.html> (Accessed July 10, 2015).

Rainer, Thom S. "What Happens When Boomer Pastors Retire?" *ThomRainer .com* <http://thomrainer.com/2014/09/happens-boomer-pastors-retire/> (Accessed December 5, 2015).

Shortsleeve, Cassie. "Why Millennials Just Aren't That Into McDonald's," *Yahoo.com*, <https://www.yahoo.com/health/why-millennials-just-arent-that-into-mcdonalds-126035358772.html> (Accessed August 20, 2015).

Stetzer, Ed. "The Rapid Rise of Nondenominational Christianity" *Christianity Today.com* http://www.christianitytoday.com/edstetzer/2015/june/rapid-rise-of-non-denominational-christianity-my-most-recen.html (Accessed February 3, 2016).

Zimmerman, Ann. "Costco CEO to Step Down," *Wall Street Journal*, <http://www.wsj.com/articles/SB10001424053111190389590457654 4883964721042> (Accessed June 10, 2015).

Made in the USA
San Bernardino, CA
04 September 2018